jimi and me

jimi and me

The Experience of a Lifetime

JONATHAN STATHAKIS

with CHRIS EPTING

PERMUTED
PRESS

A PERMUTED PRESS BOOK

Jimi and Me:
The Experience of a Lifetime
© 2023 by Jonathan Stathakis
All Rights Reserved

ISBN: 978-1-63758-811-6
ISBN (eBook): 978-1-63758-812-3

Cover design by A. J. Gentile
Front and back cover photos by Jonathan Stathakis
Insert photos Courtesy of Hey Joe, LLC. All Rights Reserved.
Interior design and composition by Greg Johnson, Textbook Perfect

PERMUTED
PRESS

Permuted Press, LLC
New York • Nashville
permutedpress.com

Published in the United States of America
1 2 3 4 5 6 7 8 9 10

To John Driver,
who gave me the confidence and motivation
to tell my story and who provided the guidance
I needed to make it happen.
I couldn't have done it without him.

Contents

Introduction

This is not a biography of Jimi Hendrix. It is not a third-party researcher's take on Hendrix. God knows there are more than enough of those books around. We all know the story: a poor boy from Seattle who grew up to become the greatest rock guitarist in the history of the world and then died tragically in London at the age of twenty-seven.

This is a book by someone who knew him and worked with him on a "secret" movie script, and at times was confided in by him. It includes stories from the legendary guitarist himself, told by him during the last twenty months of his life. Hendrix told almost all of them during one-on-one private moments, and they foster an understanding of the Jimi Hendrix behind the public figure—the vulnerable man behind the towering image.

This book tells some of his stories in his own words. Many of the stories are personal and can't be found in any other book. This helps complete all that's ever been written about Jimi Hendrix. In a way, some of this book about Jimi Hendrix is written by the only person who really knew him well—Hendrix himself. This is, in a sense, the "unpublished Hendrix." The final curtain, so to speak. I am here only to breathe life back into the words he left me.

For everything we know about Jimi Hendrix as a man, a musician, and an artist, he remains a fascination—an artist whose music is so distinctive, so recognizable, so remarkable that decades after his death, his albums continue to sell. Of all the American musical artists included in the Smithsonian Institution in Washington, DC, two have more space allocated to them than all the other artists combined: Elvis Presley and Jimi Hendrix. Hendrix appears to be as relevant today as he was when he was alive. A few years ago, *Rolling Stone* put his picture on the cover and named him the greatest guitar player in the history of rock music.

A review of Jimi's 2010 album *Valleys of Neptune* on the front page of the *Los Angeles Times*' calendar section states that Hendrix still generates an aura of possibility stronger than what many still-breathing pop stars can maintain. The reviewer remarks of Hendrix, "He's the lost rocker most strongly associated with the question 'What if?'" But the most important comment in the review is probably this one: "Something about his music points so strongly toward unimaginable next accomplishments that it's hard to consign him to the past." That's why Jimi Hendrix is still relevant today, in 2023. He remains one of the most astonishing talents of the twentieth century...and beyond.

His legend is written in one word: "Hendrix." Like Sinatra, Gershwin, Hemingway, Lennon, McCartney, Brando, Garbo. He is such a recognizable icon that he can be instantly identified by just his last name. There is only one Hendrix.

It's not difficult to gauge the tremendous impact of Jimi Hendrix on his time, as well as on the present. Even though his style has been co-opted so often, he has not lost his power to electrify a new listener. When Jimi Hendrix first appeared on the scene, he shook up guitar playing in a way that had not been seen since Les Paul invented the electric guitar. Along came Hendrix, and an art form was transfigured. His work has been imitated by performers for more than five decades, yet none of these musicians has obscured the contributions of the man who started it all. His gift was that great.

His story has been told repeatedly in book after book, by writers trying to explain a stranger they pretended to know. There have even been biographies by some who have claimed to have known him, and some who did, but with all of them trying to answer the same question: "Who was the real Jimi Hendrix?" Some have tried to reveal him through lurid hype, others through gossip or tell-all narratives by onetime so-called associates hoping to cash in on an old connection. And yet to this day, this very private man with a breathtaking talent, this international pop icon who exuded a musical power that still captivates, this surprisingly vulnerable figure surrounded by wretched excess, remains a mystery.

Nobel Prize–winning author Toni Morrison once said, "If there is a book that you want to read and it hasn't been written yet, then you must write it." The only thing is, I'm not the only one writing this book. Most of my work was done for mein a subconscious way by Jimi Hendrix's voice in my ear

I am honored to have known him and am blessed to be able to share a little something about him. He was an amazing talent, but more than that, he was a beautiful human being.

1

Meeting Hendrix

It all started in New York City in 1969, when I was living in a fifth-floor walk-up on Bethune Street in the West Village. The apartment was a block from the White Horse Tavern, the second-oldest continuously run tavern in the city. When you walked in there back then, it sure looked old. I think the owners purposely kept it that way. Amazingly, even today the White Horse Tavern is mostly physically unchanged from its 1940s, '50s, and '60s heyday. That's why I hung out there.

The White Horse opened in 1880 and was nothing more than a longshoreman's bar until the early 1940s, when it gained a reputation for being a haven for left-leaning writers, communists, and union organizers. Then in the 1950s and '60s it became a major bohemian hangout. Just about every literary luminary in Greenwich Village hung out at the White Horse, including Beat poet Allen Ginsberg, Norman Mailer, Hunter S. Thompson, James Baldwin, Anaïs Nin, William Styron, Jack Kerouac (who has the unique distinction of being thrown out of the tavern more times than any other person), and, of course, the notorious Irish poet Dylan Thomas, whom Bob Dylan credited for giving him his name. Dylan Thomas literally died there soon after his record-breaking whisky binge; he guzzled his final drink at the White Horse Tavern. Musicians also hung out there, including The Clancy Brothers, Bob Dylan, Jim Morrison, and Mary Travers of Peter, Paul and Mary. Jimi Hendrix, when he was a struggling musician playing at Cafe Wha? on MacDougal Street, where he was later discovered, also went to the tavern a couple of times, mostly sitting at the end of the bar, a complete unknown keeping to himself.

The White Horse Tavern was my local hangout. The only reason I was in my apartment on that fateful day was because I was meeting a photographer friend at the White Horse. Rather than go out, I decided to stay in until my meeting. If I had gone out, I would have missed the call.

As I was leaving my apartment, the phone rang. I stopped in the doorway, deciding whether to answer it or not. I was late for the meeting. That split-second decision to answer the phone changed my life, and I often ponder what my life would have been like if I had ignored it, closed the door, and left.

I answered the phone on about the twelfth ring. (This was well before voicemail, and I didn't have an answering machine.) The voice was male, young, a little icy.

"Jonathan Sta-*a*-kis?" he said, mispronouncing my name.

"It's Sta-*tha*-kis. Who's this?"

"We represent an artist who would like to meet you."

"I'm sorry...what?"

The guy on the phone was insistent; he had a purpose and wouldn't take no for an answer. "We want you to come over to our office. *Now*."

"*Now?*"

"Yeah, now."

It was phrased like a demand, and I didn't appreciate that. "Are you kidding me?" I protested. "Really? Who's the artist?"

Long pause.

"I can't tell you that," he finally said. "It's sensitive information. I work for him. All I can tell you is that it will be worth your while. Besides, there could be a job in it for you."

Those magic words did it. They were all I needed to hear. I decided that after the call, I would immediately cancel my meeting. Jobs for me didn't grow on trees.

"Okay, sure. I'll be there. Where?"

"East Thirty-Seventh Street, off Madison Avenue."

"Okay, yeah, and the address is?" I asked.

Again, a long pause.

Then: "Someone will meet you at Thirty-Seventh and Madison, northeast corner."

"How do you know what I look like?"

"We know."

Jesus Christ, I thought. *What is this, the Mafia?* Little did I know how prophetic that notion would prove to be.

"Fine, I'll be there," I said. "In about twenty minutes, alright?"

"Yeah."

As soon as I hung up, I called and canceled my meeting, and then I hurried out the door and I thought, *Timing—how fragile.* Although I didn't know yet that a missed call would have meant the biggest missed opportunity of my life, I knew that if I had left five minutes earlier, I would have missed *some* kind of opportunity. On the way down the stairs, I promised myself I would buy an answering machine.

Usually, I wouldn't take a taxi across town (too expensive), but there was no other way to get quickly from Bethune Street to the Turtle Bay area. In the cab, I tried to figure out who this "artist" was and why this person could be interested in meeting me. I had no clue whatsoever.

When the cab pulled up at Thirty-Seventh and Madison, I tossed the two-dollar fare at the cabbie (yes, that was including tip—it was 1969). A guy standing on the corner walked over to the cab.

One look and I knew this wasn't about the mob. This guy was, like me, in his early twenties, and had hair below his shoulders. He was wearing beads and a T-shirt with a peace emblem. He looked like every other hippie kid in New York City at the time, including me, both being in our early twenties.

"You're Jonathan?" he said.

"That's me."

"I'm G. Come on, we're just going down the street."

G.? That's his name? I thought. *Okay, sure. Why not?* Halfway down the street, G. stopped and then headed up a double-wide set of gray stone stairs to a 1920s brownstone. He opened the door for me.

"Is this a business?" I asked.

A female voice from behind the door said, "Yes. And we don't take solicitations."

I turned, saying, "Hey, you invited me."

In front of me stood an angelic young woman, a vision of haughty physical perfection. I would later learn she was named Kathy and was twenty-three years old. For me, this was a life-changing moment; I was smitten, though I did everything possible not to show it.

She asked G., "Who is this person?"

"The guy, you know, who Bob called. You've been trying to find him."

Kathy then uttered a French phrase I didn't understand but sensed was a put-down. It didn't matter. Her cultured, unapproachable personality had me. I was smitten. Suddenly, she was a must-have in my life. But just like that, she whirled and walked away to the back of the building.

"Who was that?" I asked G.

"That's Kathy. Pain in the ass."

I followed him into a waiting area on the first floor. There was nothing on the walls to identify the kind of business the place was involved in. After a few minutes, I was ushered into what looked like a lawyer's office.

There was a mahogany desk, large for the room, with piles of papers and many more stacks of folders, along with file cabinets and a typewriter. The room didn't seem like the office of a guy in charge—more like the office of a person who actually did a lot of the work. Behind the desk on the wall were framed gold records and some *Billboard* magazine articles.

Okay, this has got to have something to do with the music business, I thought. I was too far from the wall to read the names on the gold records, but before I could get up to look at them, in walked a man who introduced himself as Bob Levine. Medium height, heavyset, with almost a chrome dome, he seemed the perfectly cast lawyer, except for the fact that he wore a white shirt open at the collar instead of a jacket and tie. He seemed old to me—he had to be almost forty. Ancient in those days.

He sat down and didn't waste any time. "I'm in charge of merchandising here, and I also manage clients. One of my clients wants to meet you."

"Does your client have a name?" I asked.

5

Levine ignored the question but was quite polite. "Yes, he does. I want to thank you for coming here on such short notice. There's someone downstairs who wants to meet you. He wants to talk to you."

"Can I ask you something? How did you find me? How did you know where to look for me?" I asked.

He reached over to the credenza behind him, turned, and dropped a telephone book on the desk in front of me.

"Ma Bell. We figured there weren't too many people with your last name here, so we simply looked you up in the phone book, and there you were...the only one."

I'm glad I never got that unlisted number, I thought.

He motioned to G. to take me downstairs.

What the fuck is going on here? Should I leave? I wondered.

The downstairs area was a large space arranged like a living room, with an extensive record collection on one side and a huge stereo system on the other. When I entered, I immediately saw Jimi Hendrix. He was sitting on a four-legged black stool in the middle of the room fifteen feet in front of me, eyes closed, playing the blues on a twelve-string guitar, lost in the music. I stood frozen, transfixed, realizing I was looking straight at Jimi Hendrix.

I had his albums, but I had never seen him in person. Had never even seen him in concert. I *had* seen the *Monterey Pop* documentary. Had seen Hendrix playing his guitar behind his back and with his teeth, and—during an out-of-control rendition of "Wild Thing"—pouring lighter fluid on his guitar, burning it, and then smashing the hell out of it while it was still on fire, creating major auditory and visual impact. Rock stars had smashed guitars onstage before, but no one had ever set one on fire.

Jimi glanced up at me but didn't say anything, then went back to playing. I didn't really know what to do. I didn't know what was expected of me, and I definitely didn't feel right about interrupting. I was just completely hapless. I didn't know then that Jimi almost never started a conversation himself.

What in God's name could Jimi Hendrix, arguably the biggest rock star in America, possibly want with me? I didn't have a clue. What had I done in my brief, meandering pathetic career as a wannabe filmmaker/writer that had gotten me this front-row seat for this solo performance? Some of my friends would have given me their girlfriends for the night just to be here.

I kept saying to myself, *This is Jimi fucking Hendrix*, and stood there staring at him. Gawking is probably more like it. I remember it like it happened yesterday. It's something you don't forget. Jimi's Afro was covered by a cool black wide-brimmed hat, and he had on the perfectly fitting black velvet bell-bottom pants and black Beatle-like boots that were part of the rock star's uniform of the day. He wore a black jacket that was cut a little like a jean jacket and a little like a waiter's jacket. He looked amazingly cool. Trying to hide the fact that I was totally mesmerized, I sat down on a long couch against the wall and allowed myself to be captivated by him.

It's impossible to describe just how good a player Hendrix was. Here he was playing an acoustic guitar and was able to do anything and everything with it, apparently with no conscious effort. Sound and emotion had a direct connection with him, visceral and intense. He was not some extroverted rock star type, but someone so into music and his own sound that nothing else mattered. He wasn't just off in a zone somewhere while he played; he seemed like he was in a parallel musical universe. He was the genuine package.

I noticed that he had unusually long, perfectly formed fingers. Strong in a spider-like way. They circled the neck of the twelve-string with total assurance, like this was some comfortable childhood toy he had held all his life. I would come to learn that he held every guitar the same way.

Jimi's eyes opened again. He saw me, finished playing, and put the guitar down next to him.

Now what? I had no clue what to say or do, and he wasn't helping. Finally I got up the courage to say, "That was great. I didn't know you're into the blues."

Right after I said it, I realized I should have given my comment a little more thought; it made me seem like an asshole. To my surprise, though, he responded graciously.

"Yeah, I am," he said in almost a whisper. I would come to learn that Jimi tended to be unusually soft-spoken but not slow of speech. There was a rhythm, a kind of patter, to his words, as if he were speaking to a track of musical sixteenth notes or triplets.

He reached down, picked up his guitar, and started playing the blues again. This time I realized it was for me. If I didn't know any better, I'd swear I was in a dream. I was just blown away, and I didn't hide it.

Five minutes later, just as he was ending, I decided it would be okay to move things along. I was now curious as hell. Whatever this was about, I had a mind-blowing opportunity—a once-in-a-lifetime chance to connect with a rock star messiah on the guitar. I needed to know why.

"Do you mind if I ask, what is it you want to talk to me about?" I ventured.

"A movie, man."

"Ah...yeah...aah...okay...yeah, sure." I felt like I was losing my command of the English language.

"You're Jon, right?"

"Well, yeah, Jon...Jonathan."

"Didn't you go by 'Jon' in the film?"

"Which film was that?"

"*The Awakening Urge.*"

"Oh?... Yes, yes, *Awakening Urge.*"

I was dying inside but doing everything possible not to show it. I didn't even know the movie had been released. It was such a total piece of shit.

"Sorry, I didn't think anyone could have seen it," I said. "It wasn't supposed to be released."

"You did write the movie, right?"

"Yeah, wrote and coproduced."

Jimi looked at me. "And weren't you in it? The guy on the bed?"

"Oh yeah, that was me. It was a small part. We didn't have much money to pay actors." There was no way to hide my embarrassment. I figured this was going to be over before it even began.

If I was about to go down in flames, I needed more information from him. "Where did you see the film?" I asked.

"I caught it in London. Saw it by accident. I don't even know the theater. Groupie took me to see it because she saw it tripping on acid. She figured that was the only way to see it."

"*London?* Look, you gotta understand, that was my first film. I was just—"

"I dug it."

"*Really?*"

"Man, talk about one long wild acid ride. Left me in pieces. Trippin' off the planet. You know, Lucy in the sky and all that shit."

As I was digesting this, my face must have been frozen with a dumbfounded look. I was no longer talking to a legendary guitarist but to some guy who liked a movie made by a bunch of amateurs, me included, that had somehow ended up playing in some obscure theater in London when the film should have been burned and the ashes buried in the desert. On top of that, one of the biggest rock stars on the planet had seen it and tracked me down to talk about it. What were the odds?

And of all the things to have as a calling card for the biggest rock star in America, why did it have to be one of the worst pieces of shit ever committed to film? If anyone was responsible for its being so bad, it was me.

I decided to go for it with Jimi. Nobody was going to believe this was happening to me, anyway. Besides, Jimi Hendrix could have his pick of any filmmaker in the world, even some of the greats, and here he was talking to me, because he had somehow connected with my acid trip of a film. Crazy but true.

"So do you have an idea for a film?" I asked, trying to be cool.

"No, no...but I was working on something—writing it in hotel rooms. Something trippy. For me, and to have Mitch and Noel in it, too. We would talk about it, then we wouldn't talk about it. We'd talk and not talk, and it never goes anywhere. Then I decide it's all no good, you know?"

"Oh yeah, believe me, I know. So what kind of genre do you want to do?"

"Genre?"

"Yeah. Science fiction, comedy, horror, mystery...?"

Jimi shrugged.

"I dig some of Elvis' movies. Dig James Dean. Franken-stein's cool 'cause he's somehow almost a real person. Brando, *The Wild One*. Peter Sellers—I saw *The Mouse That Roared* six times. And I like off-the-wall stuff, you know..."

"You like Westerns?" I threw it out there.

"I dig Westerns. On the back cover of my album—"

"Yeah, I know," I interrupted. "I have that album. I mean, who doesn't? With you, Mitch, and Noel all in Western outfits with guns and on horses. That's what made me think of a Western."

"Westerns are cool. People don't talk much," Jimi said.

"Show, don't tell," I responded.

"How do you mean?"

"You tell your story with pictures," I explained. "Body language, a look, and, well...music."

"Show a lot and talk a little," Jimi responded. He played a riff that felt like an ending, then set down his guitar again.

"Or," I offered, "maybe they don't say...anything."

Jimi was intrigued. "Can you really do a whole movie without anybody talking?"

"Well, Charlie Chaplin, Rudolph Valentino.... Nobody talked in silent movies," I said.

Jimi thought this over and then said in his whispery patter, "I saw an old silent movie once in a theater with some old guy at a piano sitting all alone down front just playing. Playing, playing, playing. Playing everything, all the way through that movie." I could feel the connection to this piano player Jimi had felt. It was my first glimpse of the sensitive side of this complex, one-foot-off-the-planet man, which most of the

11

world doesn't get to see. He thought for a moment and said, "But they weren't really silent."

"Not at all."

"The old guy down front, the piano player, the music spoke for the scene."

That comment triggered something in me.

"Right...the music," I said, working it out in my head. "What if we don't say anything at all? Do a film without dialogue. Or maybe just have a few words?"

Jimi shut that down. "No. Dig it, man. We're not going to need any words. Like, none. The people will be listening with their eyes and hear the words through the music."

"You know, this could be something incredible!" I enthused. "Amazing. Like the saying 'What's old is new again.' It could get some major attention."

Suddenly, out came a long, plump joint from the coffee table drawer in front of us. Jimi sat down on the other end of the couch from me, lit up the joint, and took a hit.

In those days, I was more into liquor than cannabis and used grass more as a social thing, but I had never smoked anything like this stuff. *Is this really "purple haze?"* I wondered. Then I realized there had to be something more than grass in the joint. Maybe hash? Who knows? It was my first time smoking something that potent.

"You know why this can work without using words?" he asked as I took another tentative hit.

"No, why?"

Jimi played a riff that sounded like a question and an answer. I don't know if it was because I was so high, but I could have sworn I heard dialogue as he played.

"'Cause I can make my guitar talk," he said, grinning slyly.

He had me. This could work—it would come down to his magic. I was excited. "Yeah, okay!" I said. "You know, this could be incredible. Totally unique."

I couldn't believe it. What was supposed to only be a meet and greet was now turning into a creative session for a future movie. It had to be the joint.

Jimi calmly said, "Dig. I dig it. I like it." He started playing Elvis Presley's "(You Ain't Nothin' but a) Hound Dog," only he changed the lyrics to, "You ain't nothin' but a hound dog, gettin' stoned all the time! You ain't nothin' but a hound dog..."

He was hysterically funny as he started substituting hound dog howls for the song lyrics. With each drag of the spliff, the howls got me giggling, and soon we were laughing uncontrollably. Then he would bark and follow the bark with a long wolf-like howl, all in tune with the guitar, then go into a new verse with changed lyrics. Nothing I had ever seen or heard up to that time about Jimi Hendrix would have made me think he had a sense of humor, but he did. Around his third howl, I got another case of the giggles and then he did, too. Our laughter ended the impromptu number.

Then, out of nowhere, he said, "I want a new career."

"Really? Why?"

"Long story," was all he said. Then he closed his eyes and went silent. I was already coming to understand that Jimi's conversations jumped around like that.

After a few more hits in silence, Jimi went back to the movie. "Body language.... Okay, there's a guy...on a horse, riding...slow, very slow. In the woods. Light coming down from the sky, sort of like spotlights on a stage...through the trees."

I picked this up. "You see him close. See his face."

"Then he sees somethin', somebody."

"Then you see who he sees. Maybe it's somebody he likes... or doesn't like. Maybe it's a girl."

Jimi played a riff on the guitar. "And the music is telling you what you need to know."

Putting on my writer's hat, I said, "Remember, they had title cards in the silent movies. We could do supers or something like that, you know, to move the story along."

Jimi shook his head and looked directly into my eyes. I would come to learn that this was something he rarely did, but when he did do it, you knew he was 100 percent sure about what he was saying. "No, we won't need that," he said. "We ain't going to need nothing but music. New music. Good music. Music that will talk. And nothing that can be a hit."

"Not even a few words on the screen?" I was fighting to stay lucid. Jimi's speech had started to have a crackling sound, like Rice Krispies, and his words were popping in different colors. My spatial sense had me on one of Jupiter's moons.

"No. Dig it, man," he said. "We won't need any words. None. The people will be listening with their eyes."

"Okay." I still was having doubts, but Jimi didn't let me keep them.

"You know why we're not going to need words?" he asked, before taking a long hit and exhaling slowly. "My guitar will say the words. It will talk."

After that, I don't remember a damn thing. I think we smoked and talked and smoked and talked, and maybe I passed out. I woke up the next day in my apartment, at first convinced that I had dreamed the whole thing. I didn't remember anything we had talked about while we were taking hits on the joint. Nothing. I thought I had dreamed it, but soon it all came back, and it blew me away. *God*, I thought, *it actually happened.*

Eventually I deduced that the evening had been real. But don't ask me how I got home that night. I don't know and probably never will.

2

May to Early June 1969

The week after I met Jimi, I wrestled with the idea of going down to his office and casually dropping in, saying I was in the neighborhood. But every time I started out to do it, I changed my mind, thinking it was a bad idea. I was just too scared. Then someone from the office called, asking me if I was available to stop by. I was going to play it cool but instead said, "Yes, I'll be right over."

Maybe I shouldn't have. It wasn't what I expected.

No sooner did I get there than I was ushered into Bob Levine's office, and he started questioning me about the meeting with Jimi.

"What did you guys talk about?" he asked.

"Nothing really. A movie."

As the conversation went on, I learned that Levine was a key player in Jimi's merchandising organization and functioned basically as his day-to-day manager. But the buck always stopped with the big dog—Michael Jeffery, who the stoner gofer G. told me "is no dude to fuck with, 'cause you know he's connected."

No, actually I didn't know, and I wasn't sure what he was talking about.

My first couple of meetings with Jimi led to a plan to develop a short story that I had written into a script. It was called *Avril* (ah-VREEL). The movie would be a Western that would not have one word of dialogue, only music created by Jimi to convey the emotion of the scenes. In those preliminary meetings, I found Jimi to be very shy, nice, and polite. He was nothing like his stage persona or what any of the articles I had read about him portrayed. I would even go so far as to say he was humble. A genuinely nice guy.

At the office, I would constantly run into Kathy, Jimi's smart, blonde, blue-eyed, charismatic assistant. But I think she was more than that; I think she ran the office. I was smitten by her. I knew she was definitely not interested in me. Bob Levine was her fiancé.

The genesis of *Avril* was not as smooth as I thought it would be. It started off fine, work sessions in the office basement apartment with Jimi writing "dialogue" for the script on his electric guitar. During one of those sessions, I learned that Jimi was considering collaborating with Miles Davis on the musical score. He hinted at his plans to move in a new musical direction.

It's worth noting here that whenever I asked Jimi a question, he often would answer with a response that was so wide-ranging, it was hardly an answer at all. As nice as he was, he wasn't very forthcoming with information about himself. He even once said, "I'm startin' to wonder who I can trust." Jimi also liked to chew gum, often licorice. He said it was for his breath, but I think the chewing was at times mood-related, helping keep him calm.

I decided to let Jimi know something about me, how I'd hitchhiked to Los Angeles and somehow managed to get hired by a very weird thirty-year-old producer named Neil Cross, who still lived with his parents in Santa Monica. He was into surfing movies, and the first commercial script I ever wrote was a surfing semi-documentary. I called it *Hot Dog on a Stick*, which is a surfing term. I told Jimi that the first script meeting I had with Neil, he pulled a gun and fired it in my direction. It was a blank, but it was dangerous nonetheless and scared the shit out of me. Neil thought it was funny. I didn't. He eventually ran out of money, so the movie was never finished, but it had an impact on me, and I became a surfing nut, to the point where I even got a house on the beach at Malibu.

I also had two roommates, because there was no way I could afford the rent otherwise, and they turned out to be round-the-clock party animals. The parties we threw at the beach house became legendary—so much so that I became known as "Malibu Jon," famous for throwing parties at my rented Malibu house, until there was a fire that had to be put out with pitchers of beer. We wrecked the house so badly that ultimately the owner had to demolish it. My roommates and I immediately left California for New York before the landlord could press charges.

I would go to Jimi's office as often as I could, hoping he would make some time for *Avril*. But over time the sessions became fewer and fewer, and the time we spent together grew shorter and shorter. I had been totally naive to think that Jimi would devote time to working with me on a script when he had a million other things to do that were more important, like writing music, recording, and touring. It took a while for that to sink in, and once it did, I became more withdrawn and considered whatever time I had with him to be a gift. I knew *Avril* would never be completed. That was not his priority, far from it, but I didn't give up. I must have been totally obnoxious during that time, but in a quiet, under-the-radar way.

One time I walked in on Kathy talking to Jimi about calls from people in the Black Power movement, who were demanding a meeting. Being the highest-paid individual rock star in America had put Jimi in the movement's sights, and the organizers wanted monetary donations as well as for Jimi to do events and appearances for them. It was then that I got a sense of Jimi's avoidance of confrontation; he told Kathy to tell Michael Jeffery to handle the situation. I was now starting to hear Michael Jeffery's name being mentioned more and more. Even though I was told he had an apartment on the top floor of the office brownstone, I had yet to meet him—hadn't even seen him, had no idea what he even looked like. I was beginning to wonder if I ever wanted to meet him.

After finishing with Kathy, Jimi went down to the basement apartment, and I followed him. No sooner did we get down there than he started complaining: "That group is almost impossible to deal with, particularly in London."

He went on about bringing his white British girlfriend, Kathy Etchingham, to a meeting with the Black Panthers in London. "I should never have done that," he told me. "Now they're comin' down on me hard. Telling me I shouldn't be seen with any white chicks. Look, I can understand what they're saying and why they say it. But they're like everybody else, telling me what to do and telling me how to live my life. I go out with anybody and everybody I want to go out with."

Then he said he was going uptown to Colony Records and asked if I wanted to come along. Colony Records was located at West Fifty-Second Street and Broadway. It was the place to go for music, and not just to buy an album; it had the most extensive collection of sheet music in the country, as well as every new rock and jazz album in stock. It was probably the largest music store in New York at the time, with thousands of musical scores and records. It was a favorite of the Broadway crowd and even had a mini recording studio on the premises where struggling artists could record their music. Known artists like Jimi, even Michael Jackson and Tommy Tune, would go there and no one would bother them.

Colony Records had multiple floors, so you could lose yourself somewhere in the building. As Jimi was buying a stack of albums there, I was on another side of the store striking up a conversation with a really cool girl. Right then I discovered the power of "I'm doing a movie with Jimi Hendrix." I never reconnected with Jimi; I left with her.

It was a known fact that Jimi liked to jam at various clubs in the city, improvising with whoever was playing that night, whether it was a single musician or a band. He just loved playing. Michael Jeffery was totally against it. He wanted Jimi to be paid each time he played, not perform for free. Jimi didn't care and did it anyway. One night I accidentally wandered into a club where Jimi was playing with a pretty good house band. It was a stroke of luck. I'd heard about the club from a friend. Afterward, Jimi invited the four-member house band, me and one other guy, and nine beautiful hippie girls to the Thirty-Seventh Street office for a "gathering," as the groupie get-togethers were called. Jimi often would refer to his female groupies as his "electric ladies." We all ended up in the basement apartment of the brownstone. It was late and no one was there.

That night Jimi was unusually quiet and aloof. He didn't mix in with the party going on around him. Instead, he stood facing the wall, playing his acoustic guitar, shutting everyone out. I was sitting on the floor in the opposite corner of the room smoking a joint with two of the girls. Next to us were two other girls making out with each other. A couple of the guys were so wasted that they probably had no idea what was going on.

Near Jimi on a low bookshelf was a radio. He turned it on and landed on WNEW-FM—my go-to station. It was a progressive FM rock station that had been started in 1967 and became very influential in the development of rock music in the '60s and '70s in the tri-state area. One of its most popular late-night DJs was Alison Steele, who called herself "The Nightbird." Her program would feature progressive rock artists and musicians associated with the counterculture of the time, and she took listener requests. She had a sultry voice with a uniquely soothing mellow delivery, and she peppered her program with mysticism, quiet chatter, and sometimes poetry, as well as quotes from the Bible and Shakespeare. I listened to her more than any other DJ on the radio at the time. She was so influential that years later, *Billboard* magazine established an award in her honor, The Alison Steel Award for Lifetime Achievement, but that night she had been on the air for only about a year. She was gathering quite a following, and that night Jimi picked up the phone and called her. Without identifying himself, and disguising his voice, he asked her to play "Sunshine of Your Love" by Cream. He then turned up the volume on the radio almost full blast, strapped his guitar on, faced the wall with his back to all of us, and played along with the song. Years later an instrumental version of "Sunshine" would be released on the Hendrix CD *Valley of Neptune*.

When the number was over, I watched Jimi lean his guitar against the wall, walk over to one girl, and take her by the hand, then take another by the hand. He led them into the back bedroom of the apartment, never saying a word. Another girl, who was sitting with me, got up and followed them. I never saw Jimi, or any of them, the rest of the night. I ended up sleeping in the arms of the other girl I'd been sharing a joint with. When I awoke in the morning, she was gone. Jimi's bedroom door was open, and he was gone, too. In fact, everybody was gone.

I went upstairs to the office, and there was Kathy taking charge of a situation. It was then when I learned that Kathy was a key player in the office. I totally dug the way she took charge and sometimes even behaved like royalty. When I finally sat down to talk to her, I was surprised to learn that she and Bob Levine had been living together for almost a year. But there was something kind of weird about their relationship. Sometimes I felt as if it were more like a business arrangement.

A week or so later when Jimi resurfaced at the office one night, I happened to be there. He was on his way to a recording studio—The Hit Factory or the Record Plant; I don't remember which. I had my camera with me, which I'd never brought to the office before, so I decided to ask, "Mind if I bring a camera to the studio? I want to stay under the radar."

Jimi said, "Stay under the radar? Why?"

"I don't like being seen as a hanger-on."

"You're not."

"I don't care. A lot of times I feel like one, and that's not me."

"Okay, so bring your camera. That's cool," Jimi said, and that was the end of the conversation, but every time after that I had my camera with me. I started taking pictures at recording sessions. I had shot stills for a couple of low-budget films but brushed up on my technique with a friend who was a professional photographer, Mike Viapiana. I have an eye for shooting, and I ended up getting a lot of good stuff. I was even present when Jimi formed his new band, Gypsy Sun and Rainbows, the band that played at Woodstock, and I captured them coming together in the recording studio. It's probably the only set of pictures of the formation of Jimi's new band in the studio for their first rehearsal in existence, where they all came together for the first time.

My camera became a great cover, a reason for me to show up and stick around during recording sessions, not to mention that a lot of women are into rock photographers. I was surprised to learn that Jimi had been burned by photographers in sessions. I was both flattered and stunned when I discovered that I was one of only three or four people allowed to shoot Jimi in New York recording sessions. One of the others was his drummer, Mitch Mitchell.

New York recording sessions. One of the others was his drummer, Mitch Mitchell.

One night as I was getting ready to go see Jimi at The Record Plant to show him some of the latest pictures I shot I got a call from an ex-girlfriend, Jan. Jan and I had a brief torrid relationship and it ended as quickly as it had begun, we broke up; however, we became great friends and would hang out together on occasion. She called me because she had a date in New Jersey and her transportation fell out at the last minute and she needed to get there. I was the only one she knew that was foolish enough to have a car in New York City. She pleaded with me. I couldn't believe what was happening, here was my ex-girlfriend asking me to drive to her to her date in New Jersey because she had no other way to get there. I reluctantly said yes but told her I had to stop by the Record Plant to drop off some photos and I wasn't sure how long that would take, I advised her to call her boyfriend and tell him she might be late.

When Jan and I walked into the recording studio at the Record Plant, you couldn't miss her. Jan was a tall, charismatic Norwegian blond who exuded sexuality. She knew I was doing something with Jimi but she never met him as I made a point of not introducing my friends to him, it would have been unprofessional, and downright tacky. We went into the control room and Jan positioned herself against the back wall to be as inconspicuous as possible. Jimi was in the middle of something, playing the same note over and over again, frustrated that he wasn't getting it right. Finally he took a break.

Jimi came into the control room and saw me. I waved the photos at him. He came over to me and I handed them to him saying that we can go over them some other time when he's less busy and then I turned and motioned to Jan and we walked out. No sooner did we walk out headed to toward the elevators that Jimi popped part of his body of the studio door, tapped on it to get my attention, which he did, and motioned me to come back. I told Jan to stand by the elevator and try to hold it when it arrived. I thought for sure it was about one of the pictures but instead Jimi started asking me all sorts of questions about Jan. Who is she? Where does she live? What does she do? Does she know who he is? Do I think she would like him? I stopped the line of questions and told him I will ask her. I walked back to Jan who was holding the elevator and told her to let it go. I asked her if she thinks she might like Jimi. Jan said, "I really don't know him, but I think so. Do you think he would like me?"

I walked back into the control room, repeated to Jimi what Jan said and he said that he thinks he would really like her. He was actually very shy and was hesitant about asking the next question, almost like a schoolboy, so I took over the conversation and told him there's nothing between me and Jan, she's a former girlfriend who is now a friend and I will have all his questions answered immediately. Then I went back to Jan at the elevator, grabbed her by the hand and walked her into the control room positioned her in front of Jim and said, "Jimi, this is Jan. Jan, this is Jimi. Now knock yourselves out, because I'm leaving"

Jan's date in New Jersey either wasn't that important, or she completely forgot about him because she certainly didn't try to stop me from leaving. In the elevator I was thinking about what I just experienced. It wasn't about one of the biggest rock stars in the world, but a "normal" guy too shy to ask a girl about herself. It gave me a new insight into Jimi, something I would witness many times over. It was actually endearing.

I later learned that while doing overdubs at the Record Plant the next day, Jimi spent the whole day doing numerous takes of one guitar riff to get it the way he wanted it. Jan was there, and she witnessed that Jimi's bass player, Noel Redding, was starting to have a problem dealing with Jimi's studio perfectionism. It didn't help that Noel was originally a guitar player and wanted to go back to guitar. Jimi had been doing hours of overdubs to get things perfect, and Noel got agitated and couldn't take it anymore. He complained very vocally, lashing out at everybody, and was particularly angry with Jeffery, accusing him of holding back money owed the band. Noel got in Jimi's face and said that a pile of cash had vanished and he could prove it. Jimi avoided taking sides, but you could see that Noel's complaints were getting to Jimi. So Jimi also started asking Jeffery about money.

Sometimes when Jimi had an important gig in New York City, or just wanted a change or to get away, he would stay in a hotel, usually the Pierre or the Navarro. I met him one night at the Pierre thinking we were going to do work on *Avril*, but I knew any work wouldn't last long. I expected that Carmen Borrero might be there, and that was okay; she was cool. She was nice and genuinely cared about Jimi. She had met Jimi the year before when she was a waitress at the Whiskey a Go Go on the Sunset Strip in LA. Jimi walked in with Buddy Miles, and she quit that night and left with Jimi. According to her, it was love at first sight.

As soon as I got to the Pierre, so did Devon Wilson, Jimi's beautiful African American ex-girlfriend, who refused to accept that it was over. Devon claimed she met Jimi while he was on the Chitlin' Circuit playing in Little Richard's band. She followed him to New York with dreams of becoming a model. Sadly, in New York she became involved in prostitution, then became a drug dealer. According to other stories, she first met Jimi in New York, as a nomad drifting from place to place. I never asked Jimi about her, and he never volunteered any information, but you could see that they had a real thing going.

Devon and Jimi had a strange relationship. I think it was more like codependency. Although she was originally part of Jimi's groupie entourage, she separated from the pack and eventually became one of his most trusted friends and intimate companions. Devon was always around, even after the many times she and Jimi broke up. It's been said that the relationship he had with Devon was the closest Jimi ever had with anyone. I don't know. I wasn't there enough to find out, and my interactions with the two of them together were few and far between; however, anyone could see that she was very protective of Jimi. She even procured girls and scored drugs for him. But I feel that she needs to share the blame for encouraging, almost causing, their mutual destructive lifestyle that would eventually bring about her downfall—and to some degree, Jimi's.

After one of the times they broke up, she made a name for herself as a "super groupie." She dated and scored drugs for everyone. She was linked to Eric Clapton, Mick Jagger, and even jazz great Miles Davis, whom she met through Jimi. But she kept coming back to Jimi, and he always took her back. Eventually they'd break up again...and again. To put it mildly, Devon was popular with everyone in Jimi's entourage, especially the girls because she provided them all with whatever drug they asked for, and it kept them happy. Devon was a control freak, and she was a master at controlling a situation to her advantage. She was jealous to the point of mania, and the more Jimi tried to distance himself from her, the more jealous and possessive of him she became.

Personally, I found her to be the bitch from hell. She was arrogant, manipulative, and usually high on something. Whenever I saw her around Jimi, she was demanding, difficult, and always working him for something or trying to get in the way of Jimi's relationships with other women. She clearly had a desperate need to be around Jimi, but their relationship was so fucked up that I couldn't even begin to understand it. It was as if Devon was trying to get even with Jimi for something, but I have no idea what. Sometimes it seemed as if she wanted to destroy him while protecting him at the same time.

Sometime later, as I got to know Jimi better and he opened up to me a little more, usually during the rare creative script sessions we had, he said to me, "Devon's using heroin and trying to get me hooked. It's not happening. Smoking, it's okay though."

He mentioned that Devon had been fucking several rock stars and flaunting it. He thought she was doing it to get him jealous.

"Why do you keep her around?" It was the first and only time I ever asked him that.

Jimi's answer: "Because she can score me anything I want, whenever I want."

Some people believe that the song "Dolly Dagger" is about her. The song's title supposedly refers to Devon's parallel relationship with Mick Jagger. Even the line "She drinks her blood from a jagged edge" refers to a party where she sucked blood from Jagger's cut finger while Jimi watched in the background.

Once Devon showed up at the Pierre that day, I knew nothing was going to move forward with the script, and I didn't want to be around her, so I left.

3

Creating

I loved working with Jimi when nobody else was around. That's when we could really fire on all cylinders and explore the possibilities of what this wordless film was going to be. It blew me away how intuitive Jimi was when it came to spontaneously scoring the words I was reading. It's as if his fingers just knew where to go on the fretboard. Every note that was waiting to be discovered, he would find at the perfect moment. When he locked it in, anything and everything was possible. But there needed to be no distractions. No knocks at the door from groupies or dealers. No business from the office. Just a clear and direct channel into his most creative and natural soul.

The best way to get private time with him was when he could escape to a local hotel. The office was always a crap-shoot, because so many people were coming and going. But in a hotel room, you had a chance. Of course, once word got out where he was, people would invariably overrun the place. But when he would give me a heads-up, I would drop whatever I was doing to go meet him, because I knew we had an opportunity—at least a short window—to work on our film.

As an example, we were at The Drake Hotel one night in New York, in a two-room suite with a sound system that had a TEAC reel-to-reel tape deck. Jimi was tuning his twelve-string. I sat at a table, pencil in hand, reading from my treatment.

"Okay, we're on a hill that overlooks a house. It feels like part of the land."

"Hold up," Jimi said. He turned on his tape deck, hit Record, and played a theme into a guitar mic on a stand.

I started making changes in the treatment while Jimi tried a second feel for the theme, then a third. On his fourth try, he found one he liked.

"Give me that again," he said.

As I read, Jimi underscored the words, capturing the mood with uncanny accuracy.

"We're on a hill overlooking a homestead that feels like it's part of the land. Everything is split, hewn, and fitted."

Jimi kept a rhythmic pulse going as I kept reading.

"The man who's done the work chops wood out front...."

Jimi grabbed onto the activity, using it to energize the theme.

"His daughter comes out from the house. You wouldn't call her beautiful, but she's a flower, innocent and keenly observant. She was raised by her father. The mother died a short time ago."

This grabbed Jimi's imagination, and he created a simple melody on the twelve-string that embodied the girl's character.

"We know her as Avril," I explained.

Jimi took the girl's melody into a dazzling, sparkling arpeggio.

"Suddenly a shot rings out...."

Jimi, now totally into the story, slammed in with a chord, driving it into a heartbeat riff on the low strings.

"Avril watches her father fall to the ground...."

Jimi let loose, unleashing Avril's agony in a prolonged twelve-string lick.

"A second shot reverberates. Mom falls, and Avril runs into the house...."

The heartbeat accelerated and pounded with the girl's terror.

"Avril scrambles out a window and, running as hard as she can, disappears into a grove of saplings."

Jimi reverted to the opening theme, putting it into a minor key driven by the heartbeat, then brought the scene to a finish with a stunning series of unresolved power chords.

"I don't know. What do you think?" he asked me.

"Amazing...just amazing. You nailed it, Jimi."

"But is the style okay?"

"Okay? It's fantastic. It's not Jimi Hendrix, but it's fantastic."

"It *is* Jimi Hendrix," he said. "Where I should be, where I want to be. I need to open things up, man. I gotta bring in other cats, other musicians. Maybe even Miles."

"Miles?" I asked.

"Davis."

"Sure. He would be great."

"And not just Miles. You remember that C-minor thing I did last week for the coffin scene? You know when the dirt gets shoveled down on the wooden box?" Jimi played a few bars of an eerie haunting melody. "But you know how I hear that? On harmonica. I'm thinkin' Paul Butterfield."

Wow, what a brilliant idea, I thought. On top of that, I was a big blues harmonica fan, and Paul Butterfield was the premier blues harmonica player in the world. Period. Butterfield had come of age in the Chicago blues scene, where he met Muddy Waters and many other blues greats, who gave him encouragement and opportunities, which got his career going.

I give Jimi a lot of credit for imagining this project with other people in mind. It wasn't about ego for him. It was about making the project special and satisfying. Many other artists of Jimi's caliber no doubt would have wanted to just focus on their own contributions, but that was not him. He was all about making his project special, and I could not wait to hear what Paul Butterfield would come up with.

4

Accidental Meeting

The Bitter End was a cramped little space that was probably the most famous folk club in Greenwich Village, if not all of New York City. It was a musical institution. Owned by Fred Weintraub and later Paul Colby, it started the careers of Bob Dylan; Phil Ochs; Peter, Paul and Mary; and other musicians who had spearheaded the folk music revival of the early 1960s. Beat writers including Allen Ginsberg and Jack Kerouac had spent a lot of time in the area during the Beat movement years earlier. The Bitter End was the launching pad that nurtured and promoted some of the most prominent emerging talent of the day: Judy Collins, Bob Dylan, Joan Baez, Simon & Garfunkel, Neil Diamond, John Sebastian, The Blues Project, Lady Gaga (who performed there when she was starting out as part of the Stefani Germanotta Band), Randy Newman, and Tim Hardin, to name just a few.

The Bitter End, with only 239 seats, was a venue not only for up-and-coming musicians but for struggling comedians: Woody Allen, Albert Brooks, Lenny Bruce, George Carlin,

Dick Cavett, Bill Cosby, Billy Crystal, Cheech & Chong, Lily Tomlin, Richard Pryor, Joan Rivers, and so many others. Jimi played there, but that was long before I met him. My connection to The Bitter End was partly a folk singer named Jake Homes, who years later sued Led Zeppelin for stealing his song "Dazed and Confused," but mostly the improv comedy troupe The Ace Trucking Company.

Located a few doors down from The Bitter End was a popular bar and restaurant that was a regular hangout of mine. Between sets, the artists would hang out there, or just drop in, and exchange songs, stories, and gossip. Rarely could you go in there and not bump into a couple of well-known musicians, or at least a few up-and-comers.

Such was the case on a typically hot, muggy New York summer night in July 1969, when I ducked in there to escape the oppressive weather. Besides, I wanted to see who was there. I usually bumped into someone I knew. Tonight was no different.

I joined a table and started hanging out with some friends from The Ace Trucking Company, an ensemble that was considered the most innovative comedy troupe of the 1960s (and later the 1970s). It consisted of four guys—Fred Willard, Michael Mislove, Billy Saluga, and George Memmoli—and one woman, Patti Deutsch. They were doing sketch comedy long before *Saturday Night Live* came along. At the table that night were Fred, Mike, and Billy. A friend of theirs soon joined us, a singer from Canada named David Clayton-Thomas, who had recently become the new lead singer for a popular band called Blood Sweat & Tears.

David was totally pumped, and he got us all excited because the band's second album (his first), which had come out a few months earlier, had yielded three monster hits: "And When I Die," "You Make Me So Very Happy," and "Spinning Wheel." That week the album had gone to number one on the *Billboard* chart. That was enough of an excuse for all of us to start ordering multiple rounds of drinks to celebrate. He also told us that the band had recently been booked for the upcoming Woodstock Music and Arts Fair in August. None of us knew what that was, nor did we care. We just kept celebrating the number one album in the country, ordering drink after drink. Besides, none of us had any desire to trudge up to Woodstock, ninety miles outside of New York City, just to see a concert. (Later it was moved to Bethel, New York, after the town of Woodstock refused to allow the concert to take place there; however, if you visit the town of Woodstock today, as I recently did, you'd think it took place there, as the townspeople shamelessly promote it like it actually did.)

In the middle of the revelry, Mike Mislove nudged me and, pointing, said, "Hey, by the way, turn around. Your friend is sitting at that back table over there." It was Jimi. In those days it was commonplace for major rock stars to hang out at bars and restaurants in Greenwich Village. Nobody really paid that much attention to them; in fact, many of them lived in the Village and were always around.

I stood up and made my way across the room. With the amount of alcohol I had in me, to this day I have no idea how I made it across the room to the table where Jimi was having dinner with an outrageously dressed woman who looked vaguely familiar. I hadn't seen him for a while, and we really needed to catch up and figure out where we were at with the *Avril* script, so the timing was serendipitous. As soon as he saw me coming over, he started smiling. When I reached his

35

table, he didn't introduce me to his dinner companion, and that bugged me because she looked so familiar. He immediately apologized for not being around much but assured me that we would get back to working on the script.

"Where are you? Are you in town?" I asked.

"No. I'm hanging out upstate at a house near Woodstock. We're renting a house up there to get the band together for a gig upstate next month."

He tore off a section of the white paper tablecloth, grabbed a pen that was next to his dinner companion—who had still not uttered a word; she only kept refilling her glass from the bottle of Jim Beam on the table—and he quickly wrote his name and Woodstock phone number, then handed it to me.

"Call me and come up," he said.

"Okay. See ya." I walked away. That was the only time I ever got Jimi's autograph, unintentionally written on a piece of torn-off tablecloth with his phone number, only for it to be stolen years later by an angry girlfriend of mine at the time. To this day, I regret leaving that around for her to steal—especially since his autograph and phone number could have fetched up to $3,000 on eBay.

I went back to the table and rejoined the festivities. Fred Willard turned to me and said, "It looks like she didn't say a word to you."

"Who?"

"The chick with Hendrix! What are you, brain-dead?"

He paused, looked at me, shoved a glass of booze in front of me, and said, "That's Janis Joplin."

"*What?*" I turned around and looked back at Jimi's table. Damn, that's why she'd looked familiar.

Accidental Meeting

I think at the time she was the top female rock star in the
world, along with Grace Slick and Linda Ronstadt, but that
night she was nothing more than a stoned, weird-looking girl
staring up at me with that vacant look of someone who was
well into their seventh or eighth drink. Actually, mostly she
was gazing at Jimi, although I'm not really sure she was seeing
much of anything at that point.

I looked down at the piece of paper with Jimi's name and
number, and that's when I learned about what became known
as the "Woodstock House" and later the "Shokan House"—
the mythical bucolic enclave in Shokan, New York, where Jimi
and assorted others got ready for what would become the
most famous festival in music history...only none of us knew
it at the time.

5

The Shokan House

It had been barely two months since Jimi had gotten back from his last European tour with The Experience, with a heroin bust-up in Toronto ominously hanging over his head. This was causing Jimi an untold amount of stress and anxiety, which prompted Mike Jeffery to ask Kathy to find Jimi an "escape house" in upstate New York near Woodstock. Jimi loved the idea of Woodstock because Bob Dylan lived there. Jimi had met Dylan only once, at the Kettle of Fish bar in Greenwich Village. He was obsessed with Dylan and even covered some of his songs.

So Jimi, being a self-proclaimed Bob Dylan disciple, wanted the house to be in the town of Woodstock. Jeffery had Kathy team up with Jerry Morrison—Mike Jeffery's loosely connected partner in some ventures—to find Hendrix a house. Kathy and Morrison took Jimi to see four properties around Woodstock, including a large house that the singer Johnny Winter had rented in nearby Rhinecliff. Eventually they settled on an eight-bedroom stone manor house at the end of Traver

Hollow Road, number seventy-five, four miles southwest of Woodstock. It was in the vicinity of the Ashokan Reservoir, so Jimi called it the "Shokan House."

Jerry Morrison took credit for finding it. Morrison was a shady character; some people believed he had mob connections. He was a former song plugger who'd worked for many jazz artists, including Louie Armstrong. He also had worked for the notorious Haitian dictator Papa Doc. Jeffery and Morrison renewed their acquaintance in New York in 1968. Jeffery had recently bought a large Woodstock home on the southeast corner of Lower Byrdcliffe Road, because he was in awe of celebrity manager Albert Grossman, who lived in Woodstock, and wanted to be like him. Jeffery also wanted Jimi in the same area so he could monitor Jimi's activities. Mike Jeffery reluctantly footed the bill for the Shokan House. The rent was $3,000 a month (the equivalent would be about $24,600 today).

For Jimi, a city boy from Seattle now living in New York City, it was an amazing retreat, with horses, a stable, a gatehouse, and lots of gorgeous country property to wander around on. He moved in at the beginning of the summer of 1969 to find some solitude and peace, while he started getting material together for his new album, but it wasn't the first time Jimi had "lived" in Woodstock. After Mike Jeffery had bought a mansion in Woodstock at One Wiley Lane the year before, Jimi began visiting, so much so that Jeffery gave him the use of an apartment over the garage.

Jimi was very aware that his idol Bob Dylan lived only a quarter mile away. The village of Woodstock was filled with some of the top musical talent of the day. It was magical. Jimi, mistakenly, was starting to believe that Mike Jeffery was being influenced by the spiritual vibe of Woodstock. Jeffery even convinced Jimi that he had a desire to become more spiritual and wanted to enter into the spirit of the place. There were LSD parties at Jeffery's house, with Jeffery dropping LSD with his guests, claiming to Jimi that it was his path to becoming spiritual. Jimi was already a spiritual person without the use of LSD.

While Jimi was staying in the Wiley Lane apartment, he drove into town one day and heard an old New York acquaintance jamming on the village green. It was Juma Sultan, an African percussionist. Juma was involved with the Saugerties, New York–based arts collective Group 212. Juma and percussionist Ali Abuwi had formed a loose Afrocentric group called the Aboriginal Music Society. They were always playing around Woodstock and bringing together jazz and R&B musicians that were united by a commitment to Black consciousness.

Jimi and Juma immediately reconnected and began jamming together. In one of my conversations with Juma, whom I didn't really know that well, he told me he wanted to start a new band and that Jimi was thinking about getting a house in the area. According to Juma, that's when Jimi's quest started for a "a place that could become a band house up in Woodstock."

Early on, I visited the Shokan House a few times. Since Jimi had given me the phone number, I called and he told me to "come on up." I took that as an invitation and probably outstayed my welcome, because I went up many times. While there I saw Jimi explore new musical directions. I learned later on that this was the result of Miles Davis' influence on Jimi, and it may have led to Jimi's expanding his band, the one that eventually performed at Woodstock. I didn't know that

Jimi knew Miles Davis; they came from two totally different worlds. But then again, so did Jimi and Bob Dylan.

Months later, after Woodstock, in November, I would meet Miles Davis for the first time at Jimi's new apartment in Greenwich Village. It proved to be quite an experience, but at this point I hadn't met him, and I didn't know Jimi was considering collaborating with him. Jimi's solitude lasted only a short time, about a week; eventually along came a host of wannabe musicians, friends, hangers-on, and groupies, including several beautiful women. Soon they discovered that less than thirty minutes away from New York City by car was the exquisite Peekamoose Blue Hole, with a waterfall. Jimi's houseguests would go and drop acid there. Jimi, however, preferred to go to Peekamoose when no one else was there, with only his British girlfriend. He fell in love with it. It was easy to see why. It was a piece of paradise—a crystalline blue natural swimming pond surrounded by the Catskill Forest Preserve.

Sadly, I've been told that today it's not what it used to be, thanks to the uncontrollable influx of people from New York City escaping the confines of their apartments, where they were trapped during the COVID pandemic. People were hungry to reconnect with nature, and a natural wonder like the idyllic Peekamoose Blue Hole became the perfect day trip in the outdoors, and that destroyed it. But back in the day, there were hardly any people, and there was no trash or pollution. It was unsurpassed in its beauty and serenity.

This all came about because the month before, in July, Mike Jeffery had been approached by Michael Lang and Artie Kornfeld, two inexperienced and naive concert promoters, with an offer for Jimi to headline the last day of the Woodstock Music and Arts Fair in mid-August. They were putting together the festival with two other equally inexperienced promoters. The fact that they even ended up getting it together and eventually pulling it off was a miracle. Jeffery wanted $32,000 for Jimi to perform. They didn't have it. Eventually they settled on $18,000, which made Jimi the highest-paid artist to play at Woodstock. Since he was already in the Woodstock area, it was a no-brainer. Jeffery accepted the $18,000 (to put it in context, in today's dollars that's about $140,000), and made the deal for Jimi to play at the festival, but only after the promoters agreed that Jimi would be the headliner and go on last, closing out the festival.

That only happened because Michael Lang couldn't get the performer he wanted to close the festival. Because of his love for singing-cowboy movies as a child, Lang wanted Roy Rogers to go on after Jimi and sing "Happy Trails," closing the festival. The only reason I know this is because I was in the New York office when Michael Jeffery came out of his office telling everyone around him that it was the dumbest thing he had ever heard, and if it was going to happen, he would pull Jimi from the festival. Roy Rogers turned Lang down, so Lang agreed to Jeffery's terms.

With serious misgivings, Jimi agreed to play at the festival. He decided to use it as an opportunity to put together a new band, and asked the singer Martha Veléz—who was the wife of Jimi's percussionist, Jerry Velez—to join. Martha had just returned from recording her Janis Joplin–esque album *Fiends and Angels* in London. She turned him down, telling him that it would be too much for her.

During this time, Jimi was hanging out at the Shokan House, and he began to romanticize the country atmosphere— the beautiful sunrises and sunsets and the stargazing. Jimi was inspired by many things in life, but when you put him in nature, it was on an entirely different level. He was surrounded by inspiration. The move out of the city to the Shokan House was proving to be a good one, but there still was the anxiety about the impending drug-bust court date in Toronto.

In July 1969, more people started moving up to the Shokan House. Though Jimi kept a low profile in town, it was not easy. It had nothing to do with the flamboyant way he dressed; everybody dressed unconventionally. After all, this was Woodstock during the era of the hippie. It was the 1960s. Go back to Woodstock today, as I recently did, and you'd think it still is the '60s, or a commercial version of it. Some people are still living in the past, but they now have gray hair or no hair; some are walking with canes, some with walkers. When Jimi lived there, nobody paid attention to him; however, what did make him stand out was his car. He would tear down Tinker Street in his white Corvette Stingray convertible. Nobody in Woodstock had a new Corvette convertible, not even Dylan or the members of The Band.

There was a girl named Leslie who worked for Albert Grossman. She befriended Jimi that summer. She got him to tone it down, or at least the Corvette. She got him into organic vegetables, and they both got into making their own clothes. Jimi even went with her to clubs around town to see local musicians. The feeling people around town were getting was that he just wanted to hang and not be Jimi Hendrix. People at the Shokan House said Jimi was feeling the Woodstock thing and wanted to make it work for him. Mike Viapiana, my photographer buddy, had started spending time at the house with his cameras, capturing every image he could, mostly nature shots. He told me that he felt that Jimi could never transform from an outrageous rock star to an organic-vegetable farmer. "Jimi is living in fantasy," Mike said. "There's no way that's going to happen. He needs to come back down to Earth and make music, not grow turnips."

At the house, I began to feel like one of the hangers-on. I needed to get out of there. Jimi was telling me that he wanted to "write songs about tranquility, about beautiful things." I thought he was talking about music for the script. He wasn't. He was playing Dylan records every day in the house. I was hoping these influences would make their way into the script-writing process, but that was falling by the wayside. Soon he stopped mentioning it. I had no idea what I was doing there anymore.

One day I found him down by the creek and told him I was leaving. It appeared that he didn't even hear what I'd said. Without looking at me, staring intently at the flowing water in the creek, he remarked, "I'm tired of The Jimi Hendrix Experience. I'm tired of playing with The Experience. I'm tired of being Jimi Hendrix, rock star. That's what Jeffery wants."

After that bombshell, I don't remember his exact words, but I do remember him defending The Experience. He said they were a great band, but he knew that being in it pigeonholed him; it was something Mike Jeffery wanted to continue, because the band was such a cash cow. Artistically, Jimi was feeling strapped in by the three-member ensemble. He said it was confining. Moving up to the Shokan House, he began working on expanding his musical horizons. This excited him.

However, he knew that Jeffery would become paranoid, and Jeffery did. Soon, everything Jimi did became a threat to Jeffery. Jeffery had become so accustomed to big paychecks from the festival appearances and arena shows that The Jimi

Hendrix Experience had been performing, he was paranoid that the spigot would be shut off. He had to be wondering if Jimi would ever go back to those big paydays.

Unknown to everyone at this point, The Jimi Hendrix Experience had already played its last show on June 1. It never regrouped after that. Noel quit. Jeffery watched with unease the new crew of musicians, mostly African American, who rolled up to the Shokan House. Jimi was unaware of Jeffery's unease. All Jimi knew was that he was unhappy with his dependence on his manager and had to leave him. With no control over his own finances, he constantly had to ask Jeffery for money.

"If Jimi wanted to buy a car, he had to go to him," Juma told me. "Jeffery always claimed he was broke. He [Jimi] was maintaining this whole cadre of people, and Jeffery knew it, but there was no way he could go against it." To make matters worse, it was discovered that Noel Redding may have been right; Jeffery was, in fact, siphoning Jimi's money off into a bank account in the Bahamas. One of Jimi's girlfriends, Monika Dannemann, maintained that Jeffery had even set up the heroin bust in Toronto as a warning to teach Jimi a lesson. Whether it was true or not, nobody knew. The Jeffery situation was getting out of control. It grew more and more toxic as time went on.

All of this must have been weighing on Jimi when he asked me one day at the Shokan House, "How do I get out of a management contract?"

"You get a lawyer," I told him.

"Lawyer?"

"Yeah, one you can trust. One who works for you and nobody else, only has your interest in mind."

45

"Do you know any?"

"No, but a good friend of mine, Steve—his brother-in-law is a top New York attorney. I can introduce you."

"Okay."

As I said earlier, it was time for me to leave the Shokan House; there was nothing for me there. Jimi was into his own thing, and I wasn't part of it, so I left.

I don't know if Jimi was having an identity crisis. Did he want to be Bob Dylan? Did he want to be Miles Davis? Or did he want to be Juma Sultan? One thing was for sure: He wanted to end The Experience. The brilliant, eclectic double album *Electric Ladyland* in 1968 was the start of Jimi's ambitions' taking shape. However, Jimi's infuriating perfectionism in the studio during the recording of the album frustrated Noel Redding and also had gotten to Chas Chandler, who couldn't take it anymore and quit. Without Chas in the picture anymore, that left Jimi under the total control of Mike Jeffery. In a way, Jimi unknowingly created his own mess.

One morning, Jimi went missing from the Shokan House and was nowhere to be found. Mike Viapiana called me assuming I might know something, which I didn't, so I called Kathy at the office. She said Jimi had taken off for Morocco with his closest friends and that Mike Jeffery was furious. No surprise there. Because of the charges against Jimi for the Toronto drug bust, Jeffery had to pull strings, after the fact, to get approval from the Royal Canadian Mounted Police to allow Jimi to travel outside the country.

Jimi was gone for a little over a week. Then, just as mysteriously, he reappeared in New York City, where he started to assemble musicians for his new band. By this time, Noel Redding was fed up with Jimi's recording style—his endless takes and constant striving for perfection, never satisfied, always taking it past the point of no return. Noel's patience was reaching the boiling point. Also, Noel was a guitar player who had been recruited by Chas Chandler and Jimi to be the band's bass player, and he wanted to go back to being a guitar player. On top of it all was Noel's utter dislike and contempt for Mike Jeffery. He's the one who first figured out that Jeffery was siphoning off money to offshore bank accounts.

When Jimi came back to New York, Noel informed him that he was done, and abruptly left the band. He walked out just before the start of a recording session. This happened right after I asked him if I could take a picture of him. I wanted him standing closer to Jimi and his drummer, Mitch. That didn't sit too well. Noel said, "I've had it," and left.

That night after we left the recording studio, I went to a club with Jimi and a friend of his. There was no one in the club, which we were all happy about. After several drinks, I asked him about Morocco. His face lit up as though he'd won the lottery. Jimi loved Morocco. I asked him whom he had gone to Morocco with. He said he'd gone with Deering Howe, a good friend of his, and met up with Colette Mimram and Stella Douglas, who owned a clothing store in Greenwich Village and were already there, and Stella's husband, Alan, who was a record producer.

"I only took two thousand one hundred dollars with me; that's all I had. I didn't want to ask Jeffery for any cash, because I didn't want him to stop me," Jimi said. "It was great, man. It was great!"

The Morocco trip was probably the only vacation Jimi ever took in his life, and it lasted only a little over a week. He didn't even take his guitar with him. To him, this was a vacation, a much-needed holiday. Jimi loved Morocco, absolutely loved it. From all indications, the nine days he and the others spent together in Morocco were probably the most joyous of his entire life. According to Deering, "It was the best, and maybe the only vacation he ever had."

When Jimi got an apartment in New York City later that year, the fall after Woodstock, he even decorated it in a Moroccan motif. Deering, Colette, Alan, Stella, and him had been like five peas in a pod. Jimi loved being with them because they were friends that had absolutely nothing to do with the music business, with the exception of Alan. And Stella had been born in Morocco. During the last years of Jimi's life, she became one of his closest friends.

I had been to Stella and Colette's clothing store only once, but Jimi was there often; in fact, they designed many of Jimi's outfits that he wore onstage, including the famous turquoise beaded jacket with white fringed that he wore at the Woodstock festival. Jimi even named their shop for them: The Nudist Colony. (He'd originally suggested calling it Band of Gypsies.) Jimi loved that Colette, Stella, and Deering were more cultured than he was, and he loved their great fashion sense. Jimi developed his first real adult friendships outside the music industry with those three.

After Jimi left Morocco, people there told stories that were mostly fictitious. They claimed that Jimi came back to Morocco later on because he loved it so much. True, he did love it, but Jimi only went once, flying there on a regular commercial flight. He told me he stayed at three hotels in three cities but mainly at the Hotel Des Iles in Essaouira, even though managers of other hotels falsely claimed he stayed at their hotels. There was also a restaurant that claimed he ate there regularly while in Morocco, but the restaurant didn't exist in 1969 when Jimi was there. What was true was that Jimi loved Casablanca.

6

Gypsy Sun and Rainbows

Back in NYC, Jimi started putting a new band together, recruiting three of his old friends. A former Army buddy Billy Cox was a rock-solid bass player and someone Jimi used to jam with during their time in the service; in many ways he was better than Noel. Billy was also a great influence on Jimi because he didn't take drugs, was levelheaded, and was the rock Jimi needed, someone he could trust and lean on. Another Army buddy, Larry Lee, a rhythm guitar player from Memphis, had just gotten back from serving in Vietnam and joined the band. Jimi told me that both Billy and Larry had been with him in the early '60s, playing in rhythm and blues groups.

Having the two of them, especially Billy, helped Jimi focus. And, of course, he had Juma. Jimi needed people he could trust and feel comfortable with, and Billy, Larry, and Juma fit the bill. Eventually Juma moved into the gatehouse at the Shokan House with his Chinese American girlfriend, and they soon installed themselves as a permanent fixture there. Jimi added another local Woodstock musician, conga player and jazz fusion percussionist Gerardo "Jerry" Velez, to the band.

When Experience drummer Mitch Mitchell showed up one day, Jimi really got a sense of just how multifaceted his new band could be. Mitch originally had been a jazz drummer, and he never really lost his fondness for jazz. He was the perfect drummer for the new band, and Jimi knew it. Mitch was an iconic drummer. He had an explosive energy all his own.

This was the first band that Jimi formed that showcased Black musicians—four of the six members were Black—and it became evident to me that Jimi was exploring the kind of avant-garde Afro-jazz-rock sound espoused by Juma, who dressed in robes and who was pushing Jimi to explore the fusion of jazz and tribal percussion.

They all gathered at The Hit Factory recording studio in New York City, where Jimi could start teaching them the songs they were going to perform at Woodstock. To make up for canceling the script work sessions we had planned, Jimi invited me to The Hit Factory. I showed up with my camera and my photographer friend, Mike Viapiana. Although we didn't know it at the time, the pictures we took were not only the first ones ever taken of Jimi rehearsing his new band for the Woodstock festival. Except for a couple of photos taken by Mitch, they are the only pictures in existence of the birth of Gypsy Sun and Rainbows. I heard that some of Mitch's photos ended up in a book he wrote.

Jimi went from player to player, showing them the chords, teaching them the songs.

After we left The Hit Factory, some of us went with Jimi to a local bar on Ninth Avenue and had drinks. After a while, I asked Jimi his feelings about the upcoming concert. Jimi said that it was his destiny to play Woodstock.

I looked at him. "Destiny?"

"Yeah, man, because the tarot card lady said I'm gonna be appearing in front of a big crowd."

I pointed out that he usually played for big crowds, and he could do it every week if he wanted to.

"No, this is gonna be some gigantic gathering, like half the planet," he said.

Jeffery had already made the deal for Jimi to perform and had gotten the money up front. After Jeffery cashed the check, he was elated to have gotten Jimi's fee up front—because, as he commented, "Who will want to drive two hours to the middle of nowhere to see a concert?"

Jimi did not return to The Hit Factory to continue the rehearsals. Instead, he moved everyone up to the Shokan House to hang out, ride horses, and rehearse. I called and asked if I could visit; thereafter I would occasionally show up, but only if I wasn't intruding.

Jimi started applying a meditative approach to his songwriting, à la Bob Dylan and Woodstock. He was a very smart and extremely sensitive person who felt that he was getting trapped in his own creation, and that it was necessary for him to break out, but it had to be totally on his own terms. To do that, he had to have a space where there wasn't a lot of observation, and that was the Shokan House. Mike Viapiana told me that after I left to go back to New York for a while, Jimi went about creating a name for his new band. He wanted it to be Electric Sky Church, which was a reference to the fact that the house sat high above the Ashokan Reservoir, but then he inexplicably changed the name to Gypsy Sun and Rainbows.

Mitch thought the band was terrible, that it lacked cohesion and direction. He was accustomed to the tight pop, three- and four-minute rock 'n' roll structures of The Experience. The new band was about improvisation and exploration. And Mitch saw that Jimi was floundering in his new role as improvisatory band leader. I wasn't there and didn't witness it, but Mitch said that during one jam session at the Shokan House, Jimi became so frustrated that he flung his guitar across the room. Jimi was always asking others in the band how they were coming across. Most told him they liked what they heard, but not Mitch. One time he commented to the others, "Sometimes it doesn't sound like you're all playing the same number." Leave it to Mitch to be blunt.

Someone called to tell me that Jimi had set up a meeting with Paul Butterfield, the blues harmonica player, and that I had to get to Woodstock for it. The person said, "You need to go meet with Paul Butterfield; he's at the Little Bear. He's got some music he recorded that he wants you to listen to; it's for the movie." That was all I needed to hear. I dropped everything and drove up to Bearsville, where the Little Bear, a bar-restaurant, was located. The drive normally took almost three hours, but I did it in two.

Jimi had introduced me to Paul Butterfield sometime before, and I'd told Paul about the concept for the movie—no dialogue, speaking through music. He loved the idea and offered to demo some tunes for it. I was all for it. I found it interesting that Jimi chose to put me together with a blues artist. I wondered if he was thinking of using the movie to reconnect with his musical heritage.

Over the years it has been forgotten that it was Paul Butterfield who inspired Bob Dylan to plug in. It all happened at the Newport Folk Festival on July 23, 1965. At the time Paul Butterfield, a virtuoso harmonica player, was leader of a multi-racial bunch young early 20-year-olds making their first appearance at the festival. His blues band was led by a guitar prodigy, Mike Bloomfield, and co-founder rhythm guitar player Elvin Bishop. The band delivered a knockout performance, especially Butterfield. As it turned out, one of the performers that weekend who chanced upon the group was Bob Dylan.

After witnessing an incredible performance by Paul But-terfield's band, Bob Dylan made the decision to go electric, and not only did he go electric, he used the Paul Butterfield Blues Band to back him during his historic, and controver-sial, Newport Folk Festival headlining set that Sunday. It was a decision that changed Dylan's career, and music, forever. It can be argued that the Paul Butterfield blues Band's perfor-mance at the Newport Folk Festival was just as influential as Bob Dylan's in that it was the catalyst that changed the trajec-tory of pop music forever. I was in awe of Paul Butterfield and blown away that he could be a part of this project.

I met Paul at the Bear Cafe in Bearsville, a hamlet two miles outside of Woodstock. It was the place to go for local musicians. It was started and owned by Butterfield's manager, Albert Grossman. Grossman, who lived in Bearsville, was con-sidered one of the most influential managers of musical talent at the time. He had a knack for finding unique talents and man-aging their careers, and managed many of the most popular and successful artists in folk-rock music: not only Paul Butter-field but Gordon Lightfoot; Odetta; Ian & Sylvia; NRBQ; Todd Rundgren; Janis Joplin; Peter, Paul and Mary; The Band; and his most famous client, Bob Dylan. Grossman's wife, Sally, was immortalized on the cover of Bob Dylan's album *Bringing It All Back Home.*

Grossman owned most of the town of Bearsville. He was once referred to as rock 'n' roll's Citizen Kane. Most of the artists lived in the Woodstock area because of Grossman. They formed a sort-of upstate New York artists' colony. He was also the owner and founder of Bearsville Records and Bearsville Studios. When he died in 1986, Grossman was buried behind his own Bearsville Theater, next to the cafe. As controversial as he was for being a tough manager who played outside the box and used controversial strategies to get what he wanted, one thing that everyone agreed on about Albert Grossman was that he redefined the role of personal manager in the music business, and in the process, profoundly changed the nature of both popular music and the music business itself.

At the cafe, once we settled in, Paul played a tape recording of the music he'd created for the film. He was arguably the best blues harp player in the world. The harmonica sound effects sounded like pebbles falling on a coffin, which exactly captured the emotion of the scene he had created the sound for. I was so excited—the music was interesting and different—that instead of driving back to New York City, I went straight to the house and played it for Jimi. Jimi was intrigued, but I suspected he was almost envious of Paul's freedom to make the kind of music he wanted, something Jeffery had prevented Jimi from doing.

In fact, some of the musicians who gathered up at the house told Jimi stories about how Jeffery had pressured them to discuss what their intentions were with Jimi. They didn't like that. They just wanted to jam and be with Jimi, whom they considered a friend. They were not interested in Jeffery's hypersensitive and insecure inquisitions regarding Jimi. And Jimi didn't really give a shit what Jeffery thought. He was into trying new things. He was all about the moment and what he could do with his ever-growing musical tribe in Woodstock, Boiceville, and Saugerties.

When I was at the Shokan House, some of the musicians who came around were Paul Butterfield and members of his band, Rick Danko and Levon Helm of The Band, Tim Hardin, and Janis Joplin. Some came to the Tinker Street Cinema in Woodstock, where the band often rehearsed. The Paul Butterfield Blues Band also rehearsed at the theater. The Tinker Street Cinema was a former pre–Civil War Methodist church that had been converted into a movie theater in1961 by a local motel owner. It was the only theater in Woodstock. Gypsy Sun and Rainbows jammed nightly at the Shokan House but rehearsed at the Tinker Street Cinema.

On August 10, 1969, Jimi began rehearsing the band in earnest. They performed as a band for the first time at Tinker Street. To give you an idea of how happening the Woodstock music scene was at that time, on the same night that Jimi held a jam session at Tinker Street, Johnny Winter was playing nearby at the Café Espresso; Santana, an unknown rising star at the time, was playing at the Elephant Club; and Van Morrison was at the Sled Hill Café, where he sang with a local band. Jimi didn't visit any clubs. He was focused on his new band.

When I got back to the Shokan House after the Paul Butterfield meeting, I could see that Jimi was inspired and fired up about rehearsing Gypsy Sun and Rainbows. I knew he had no time for me, so I drove back to the city.

7

Michael Jeffery

As soon as I walked into my NYC apartment and collapsed on my couch after returning from Woodstock in July 1969, Kathy called from the office.

"You have to go up to Woodstock," she told me.

"What? I just came from Woodstock."

"Well, you have to go back."

"Kathy, c'mon, what do you mean I have to go back? Why?"

"Jeffery wants to see you at his house today," she said.

"Today? Really?"

"Yes, really." A pause. "And don't think you *don't* want to do it. Trust me on this one."

"Okay, okay. Give me the address, and can you please call him and tell him that I'm back in the city and won't get back up there until about five or six?"

The last thing I wanted to do was go see Mike Jeffery. All this time, the man had never spoken more than six words to me and had never interacted with me. Why now?

Driving back up to Woodstock, I replayed in my mind all that I knew or had heard about Mike Jeffery. I had plenty of time to go over it, since it was about a three-hour drive. Here's what I thought about.

Everyone knows that Chas Chandler discovered Jimi, then known as Jimmy James, at Cafe Wha? in New York and took him back with him to London and repackaged him as Jimi Hendrix. Chandler was convinced that Jimi was the greatest guitarist he'd ever heard, and time has proven him right. Chandler also knew that he didn't have the finances to fund Jimi in the U.K., or the resources to secure a recording contract for him. So, knowing he needed a partner to help him with the finances and the know-how to launch a career, Chandler went to Mike Jeffery, the manager of the band Chandler was in, The Animals. He did this despite the way Mike Jeffery had ripped off The Animals.

Chandler was still under contract to Jeffery, which meant that Jeffery would have a claim to a portion of any money he earned with Jimi if Jimi were to become successful. Jeffery agreed to the partnership and offered to throw the New Animals, a band formed to replace the original Animals who had broken up, and Alan Price (also a former member of The Animals and now a solo artist) into a pool of artists that he and Chandler would manage together. Chandler and Jeffery formed a management company.

And that's how it began. Jimi went to London.

In London, Chandler and Jeffery decided to build a band around Jimi. Being a big fan of Cream, Jimi wanted the same lineup—three instruments: a guitar, a bass guitar, and drums. Noel Redding, a guitarist, became the bass player, and Mitch

Mitchell became the drummer. The group was named The Jimi Hendrix Experience.

The band signed a contract, which was more like a production deal, whereby Mike Jeffery and Chas Chandler would be record producers. I know this because when Jimi asked me for some help in getting out of his contract with Jeffery, Kathy snuck me a copy of the signed contract and it was not a management contract; in fact, there was nothing in the contract to indicate a differing status among Jimi and Noel and Mitch. They were all merely individual musicians collectively known as The Jimi Hendrix Experience. Mike Jeffery and Chas Chandler were granted a 20 percent cut of earnings plus further percentages for royalties and publishing deals. All the members of The Jimi Hendrix Experience, collectively, would share 2.5 percent of royalties from record sales. This was not a very favorable deal for Jimi, but at the time none of the band members had any idea how successful they would become, not even Jeffery. Although I think Chas Chandler might have known.

Later, when Jeffery realized what he had in Jimi, he changed the contract to reflect Jeffery's take at 40 percent of Jimi's gross performance earnings—a staggering percentage! The only other contract in existence like it that I'd ever heard of was between Elvis and Colonel Tom Parker, who took 50 percent of Elvis' earnings. Forty percent was a huge amount by show business standards; even 20 percent would have been pushing it. Mike Jeffery justified it by explaining that part of that percentage would pay for touring expenses. Jeffery took advantage of Jimi's lack of business experience and set up various bank accounts in the Bahamas, convincing Jimi that if he did well, those accounts would save Jimi from paying too much in taxes, and he would have more than enough money to support himself for the rest of his life.

Jeffery didn't offer Jimi the opportunity to seek his own independent legal counsel. Also, Jeffery conveniently never discussed with his "partner," Chas Chandler, the contract meeting he'd had with Jimi. The agreement that Jimi signed with Jeffery seriously affected him for his entire career.

A short time after the band was formed, The Jimi Hendrix Experience did a brief tour of select European countries, and it turned out the cost far outweighed the income. Chas Chandler began to worry about expenses. Not only that, but Noel and Mitch were already unhappy about the small amounts they were receiving in wages—yes, actual payroll wages—and were complaining to Mike Jeffery. Neither Noel nor Mitch had signed a contract with Jeffery; theirs was a verbal agreement. And, as such, Jeffery treated them as employees. Mitch stuck it out, but the seeds of discontent were already beginning to grow in Noel early on.

On top of everything else, The Jimi Hendrix Experience was rehearsing and playing with equipment that none of the band members were happy with. It affected their performances and their sound. It came down to money that was needed to buy better equipment, and Chandler was relying on Jeffery to supply the investment needed to establish The Jimi Hendrix Experience. Jeffery told Chandler that all his money was tied up in litigation involving The Animals, which wasn't entirely true. At the time, he was running several nightclubs in Mallorca, Spain, and making a ton of money. What it all came down to was that Jeffery didn't have the faith in Jimi Hendrix that Chandler had. Eventually, Chandler had to sell most of his bass guitars to provide the money for better equipment for The Jimi Hendrix Experience.

At this point, they needed a record deal to get some money in. Jeffery and Chandler knew that they couldn't expect much money from a record company as an advance against future royalties, but even a small amount would help. Jeffery met with Decca Records A&R (artists and repertoire) man Dick Row to get a record deal. Why Jeffery picked Rowe is a mystery because Rowe had once turned down The Beatles when they were offered to him. Maybe Jeffery figured Rowe would not make the same mistake twice. This was not the case, however; Rowe turned down Jimi Hendrix, telling Jeffery that he thought Jimi was lacking in long-term potential. If Decca didn't fire Rowe after Jimi made it big, then Decca deserves to have missed out on both The Beatles and Hendrix, because Rowe was truly tone-deaf.

I don't know all the behind-the-scenes games that took place, but I believe that Jeffery does deserve the credit for getting the song "Hey Joe" released—which no doubt was the result of every underhanded trick Jeffery was capable of. It's rumored that Jeffery engaged in what is known as chart-rigging, and if he did, it worked. Jimi found out later that Jeffery also did a deal with a consortium of pirate radio stations to ensure that "Hey Joe" would get continuous airplay. He paid a heavy price, in that he traded a percentage of Jimi's future publishing royalties for the exposure, something that would come back to haunt him and Jimi.

By the time The Jimi Hendrix Experience arrived in the U.S., one of the lawyers working on behalf of Jeffery secured a record deal with the Warner Brothers label Reprise. But I learned from Kathy, who was a wealth of information, that the contract completely bypassed The Jimi Hendrix Experience and was actually between Reprise Records and Mike Jeffery and Chas Chandler's management company. Their management company was required to provide only recordings "embodying the performance of Jimi Hendrix or The Jimi Hendrix Experience."

Mitch and Noel were exclusively tied to the Jeffery/Chandler management company, so they couldn't sign anything, and as part of the agreement, the management company, not Reprise, retained the ownership of Jimi's master recordings. The managers got a $150,000 deal, a royalty advance of $40,000, and a promotional budget of $20,000. This was not a great deal for the band members, but it was for Mike Jeffery and Chas Chandler in the end.

There's more. The contract allowed Jeffery and Chandler to arrange any production or publishing deals they wanted to, and they did. The members of the band had nothing to say about it. The production contracts Jeffery and Chandler entered after that paid them an 8 percent royalty on record sales, but the band got nothing—*nothing*. Then, on top of that, Jeffery did a side deal with British record label Polydor, whereby all the rights to The Jimi Hendrix Experience's works would revert back to him and Chandler once the previous contract had lapsed. Even being a somewhat inexperienced kid with a camera at the time, I knew that this sucked, and that the band was fucked. No wonder Jimi wanted to get out of his contract with Jeffery.

It's not surprising that the band members were far from happy. I felt like a fly on the wall hearing them complaining about the small amounts of money they were being given. All three of them were paid very poorly. Noel wrote a letter to Jeffery and Chandler, which Mitch and Jimi signed, laying out their grievances. In a brilliant move, Jeffery temporarily bought them off with some instant cash in hand. What he didn't know was that the three members of The Jimi Hendrix Experience now had an oral agreement between them to split everything on a 50-25-25 basis, with the 50 being for Jimi. I wasn't around when all of this was going on. I learned of it during one of the writing sessions I had with Jimi. I began to understand why he wanted Jeffery to know as little as possible.

So here I was driving up to Woodstock, again, going over these things in my mind. Why? I don't know. Maybe to paint a clear picture in my mind of the person I was going to meet, because I had no idea why he had summoned me. Yes, he'd seen me around the office, but he'd never approached me or even said hello. He'd hardly even acknowledged me, but then again, why would he have?

Unbeknownst to him, Kathy had let me read some business-related documents. I'm not sure why she did, and most of what I saw, I've forgotten. I wasn't really that interested at the time, more curious than anything else. I think if Jeffery knew that Kathy had let me read the contracts, he would have killed us both. When that thought entered my mind, I started to freak out, but I did my best to keep my cool, as I was driving seventy-five miles an hour on the New York State Thruway.

All I could think of was the stories I heard about Mike Jeffery. He'd served in the British National Service, enlisting as a full-time soldier. Around the office and elsewhere, there was a lot of speculation about Jeffery's involvement with other government agencies. Some people have suggested that he worked for the British Secret Service. Lots of different theories have been published either in books or on the internet. But in those days, there was no internet, so it was almost impossible to check him out. I went with what I heard depending on whom I'd heard it from.

Apparently, Jeffery was a gifted storyteller who told people about his time in the British Army and his exploits as an undercover operative, especially the people around the office, either to boast or to intimidate them, or maybe both. Of course, it didn't faze Kathy; she didn't give a shit. She thought his stories were fabricated or greatly exaggerated, told not only to amuse his listeners but also to create an image of himself as a person not to be messed with. For the most part, it worked; many believed the stories were true. Up until now, I didn't care, but I was thinking that maybe I should have cared.

There was a story circulating around supposedly heard firsthand by Eric Burdon, lead singer of The Animals, that in Mallorca years before, Jeffery—who ran several nightclubs on the island—became enraged that many battleships from the U.S. Seventh Fleet were docked at the port and the town was overrun with American sailors; he didn't like American sailors in his clubs. The reason they were there, according to Jeffery, was that the U.S. had lost a hydrogen bomb off the coast of Spain and two U.S. planes collided in midair searching for it. Dozens of U.S. naval vessels were involved in the search-and-recovery mission and at one point used the port at Palma, Mallorca, as their base. Supposedly, wearing a wet suit and breathing apparatus, Jeffery swam out to the area where the ships were anchored and set up some incendiary charges near the ships, which he later detonated from shore using a handheld device, causing explosions. This resulted in the Navy's weighing anchor and leaving Mallorca. Did it really happen? Who knows? It sounded like bullshit to me. Jeffery, of course, said it did happen.

I also heard there was a guy named Malcolm Cecil, who had known Jeffery many years before, when they became partners and started the Downbeat Club in England. Cecil said that he learned that Jeffery was a high-ranking officer in the British Secret Service, and over time Jeffery managed to have Cecil hand over—maybe even forced him to hand over—his ownership in the club to Jeffery. As a result, Cecil left the club business and became a record producer. He reconnected with Jeffery years later when Cecil was working with Stevie Wonder at Electric Lady Studios.

There were other stories floating around, including Jeffery's involvement in covert operations in Communist-run Yugoslavia that may have involved kidnapping and executions, and that he was also involved in illegal military activities in the Suez. Jeffery claimed he was a member of the British Intelligence Corps and often assisted MI6 in low-key tasks such as searching for spies and liaising with the Italian intelligence service. But, as I said, there was really no way back then to check somebody out. Whether the stories were true or not, Mike Jeffery was a bad guy, and his Mafia connections were not a fantasy. He was even coerced by the Mafia into adding a band to his management roster they controlled, Vanilla Fudge. I kept my distance from that. Besides, I was a kid with a camera who was writing a Western movie. What did I know? As time went on, I knew more than I cared to admit, especially to myself.

All this was running through my mind when I pulled up to Mike Jeffery's Woodstock house at One Wiley Lane. I had never been there before, had never had a reason to. He'd built high fences around the property, which I later learned was to hide his drug activities (supposedly supplying drugs to the other musicians he had under management), his Mafia cohorts, and his out-of-control showbiz lifestyle. The gate was open, so I knew he was waiting for me.

I can picture it now as if it were yesterday, because it was my first encounter with Jeffery. I didn't know it then, but I would have only two more interactions with Jeffery, one on the stage at Woodstock and the other in a limo in front of Jimi's apartment. For some reason, these memories are more vivid than many of my memories of Jimi. Go figure. With my camera slung over my shoulder, I knocked on the door and waited.

Lyn Baily answered the door. She was a Canadian model who had come to New York from Toronto with a fellow Canadian, the musician Levon Helm. She met Jeffery when he was living in the apartment above the office in the brownstone on East Thirty-Seventh Street. They soon became lovers, and Lyn gave up her career as a model and moved in with Jeffery.

She invited me in and told me to wait in the foyer. I stood there for what seemed like an eternity. Kathy had told me that since Chas Chandler stopped sharing management duties with Jeffery, the real problem for Jimi in having Jeffery as his sole manager was that he always put money first. He needed a constant stream of money, both for himself and The Jimi Hendrix Experience (but more for himself). Observing as much of the interior of the house as I could see, I believed it. Jeffery must have spent a small fortune decorating the house, which is probably why he wanted Jimi touring—to keep the money coming in.

Interestingly, Jeffery wasn't as involved with Jimi on a personal level as was Chandler. He had other interests. Jeffery, unlike Chas, had little appreciation for the creative process and was interested only when Jimi was touring and generating large amounts of money. The money was essential to Jeffery, as the tax authorities had caught up with him, and several investors were also chasing him for money. I would later learn that Bob Levine was one of them.

With Chandler gone, Jimi lost a very important part of his direction and day-to-day care. If it weren't for Kathy running the office and acting as Jimi's personal assistant, I don't think anyone would have really looked out for Jimi.

Finally, Jeffery appeared. I think he purposely had kept me waiting, so I could conjure up all sorts of weird ideas that would freak me out by the time he appeared. Little did he know that I already had done that driving up. It was obvious he wasn't happy to see me.

"So, you don't know the fucker's run off?" he said, first thing.

I had no idea what he was talking about. "Run off?"

He turned around and started walking toward another room, obviously expecting me to follow him. He talked as he was walking, more to himself than to me.

"Morocco, with Colette. The bitch told him that her grandfather was a tribal leader. What bullshit! Deering Howe went, and so did that other bitch Stella Douglas."

I followed him into the large, high-ceilinged library, which was partially cleared and set up with instruments for a band rehearsal that had never happened. None of the musicians at the Shokan House had any interest in rehearsing at Jeffery's place.

He abruptly stopped in the middle of the room, turned, and got up in my face.

"Tell me, mister, what are these rumblings I hear about Jimi taking his music in some new direction?"

"I'm sorry, but I don't know what you're talking about. I don't have anything to do with his music."

He backed off and picked up an African drum.

"And what does he expect me to do? Fly a bunch of darkies around the world every time he does a gig? He needs to settle down, write more, and record more. Why do you think I'm spending *three thousand fucking dollars a month on Shokan*? Fuck this Black band shit. He needs The Experience with two white guys behind him! *You understand?*"

I was genuinely confused as to why he was jumping all over me, since I didn't know anything and it really wasn't any of my business. He suddenly became accusatory.

"Why doesn't anyone ever see you hanging out with Jimi?" he asked.

"I really don't hang out with Jimi. I like staying under the radar."

It was like a switch flipped in Jeffery's mind then. He became paranoid, glaring at me as if I were a threat. He pumped me about the movie project and other things going on in Jimi's life.

"Who's coming up to the house? What's happening with the band? Might I suggest we make an arrangement? You let me know everything going on that I should know about, and don't give me that under-the-radar bullshit, you bottom-feeding piece of scum. You're just like the rest of the hangers-on."

"Listen, I'm not a hanger-on, and I am not a groupie, okay? It's not me."

"Is that so?" He dropped the drum so it hit the floor with a loud bang, almost to make a point. Then he pushed his jacket aside to make sure I caught a glimpse of a .38 snub-nose revolver in a holster on his belt.

"Sit down. Now!" he barked.

I calmly sat down in the chair he positioned me in. I'd been around guns, had even owned a couple at one time, so I wasn't intimidated. I removed my camera from my shoulder and set it down on a side table.

"You don't really know who I am, do you?" he asked.

"No, I guess I don't."

"Well, sonny, let me enlighten you."

As Jeffery was talking, he circled me while I was sitting in the chair.

"I am the man who owns Jimi Hendrix. His destiny is mine. I created him. Without me, he would still be playing some bar on the Chitlin' Circuit. *Get the picture?* So why are you fucking with my Jimi?"

"I am *not* fucking with anybody, especially not you. Jimi and I have a professional relationship, that's it. We're working on a movie script, nothing more."

"A movie? Really? Like Jimi even has the time to do that? What's it about?"

"It's a Western."

"A what?"

"You know, cowboys and Indians. Horses. Guns. Oh, I forgot, you don't have that stuff in England."

"Don't you dare be sarcastic with me, you little turd!" Jeffery was shouting at me so loudly that a tall, stocky goon, his "chauffeur," came in.

"Everything okay, Mr. Jeffery?" he asked.

"Yes, thank you, Ruddy." Looking at me, he added: "Isn't it?"

"Yes. It is."

The chauffeur gave me a piercing look and left the room.

"Do you know what has to be done to get a song on the radio?" Jeffery asked me. "Do you?"

"Not really."

"I didn't think so. You need 'friends.' And friends don't like their investment to be fucked with, and neither do I." Then he yelled, "Who are you anyway? What are you?"

"What do you mean, what am I?"

"Most people shit themselves when they see a gun," Jeffery said. "You're too fucking calm. *What are you hiding?*"

"Nothing. I've got nothing to hide, nothing."

I could see now that Jeffery was paranoid, and he definitely didn't believe me. He leaned over me.

"I need you to get close to Hendrix and stay close," he instructed. "I want to know everything he does at that house, everything about the band he's put together, how to end it, and everyone I should know about. There's going to be no colored musicians. *Get it?* And then your so-called Western just might get made."

That did it. I lashed out at him: "That's not the way I work. I'm just trying to write a script with Jimi, that's all. I do the writing; he does the music. Period. There's nothing else happening. *Nothing.* I don't discuss business, and I don't ask. I don't control him. I don't tell him what to do; in fact, I hardly see him. So whatever influence you think I have over him, I don't, and I'm sure as hell not going to hang around Shokan spying on him for you. That's not going to happen, so find someone else."

I didn't know that Jeffery had already approached some of the musicians at the house demanding that they spy for him. No one wanted anything to do with him. They all turned him down. I think I was his last try, and that wasn't going too well. I got up to leave. He grabbed me and pushed me down into the seat, hard.

"Now you listen, 'cause things happen to blokes who don't listen. You *better* listen. During the war, we'd cut off their ears, and if we had the time, we'd feed them to some pet. I've squashed more than my share of little pissants to get where I am. Don't you *ever* forget that. Ever! So, you watch yourself."

He picked up my camera and dangled it in front of me.

"And if you ever, ever, ever take my picture, you'll be taking photographs with stumps for fingers. Do you understand?"

It dawned on me at that point that Jeffery might be high and that I'd better get out of there, because I had no idea when he'd taken the drugs and what drugs he'd taken. I was told he favored both LSD and cocaine, and I had no desire to stick around to find out which. I jumped up, yanked my camera from his hand, and walked as fast as I could toward the door. Fortunately, I did not pass the "chauffer," and I made it out.

I jumped in my car and spun out. In the rearview mirror, I could see that Jeffery was now in the doorway ranting. I had no idea what he was saying, nor did I want to know. All I could see was that this "proper" Brit who had a reputation for being cool and reserved was anything but, standing in that doorway red-faced and furious. Then I remembered he had a gun. I floored the pedal and didn't stop till I made it back to Manhattan.

Everything I had heard about Jeffery seemed to be true. He was intimidating. He was not to be trusted. He was controlling, an international nightclub owner, mob-connected, an ex-British spy with ties to the British Secret Service. And he carried a gun. Did I leave anything out? Probably.

8

Woodstock

I never intended to go to Woodstock. After being at the Shokan House and dropping in on a few rehearsals, I didn't feel the need to drive two hours to an outdoor festival in a place I'd never been to. I knew the actual Woodstock area and the town well, but there was confusion as to what the area where the festival had been moved to was called—White Lake or Bethel. I had no clue where either was. Besides, I was starting to be influenced by Mitch's complaints about the band. Listening to Mitch, I thought the Woodstock performance had the potential to be a disaster for them. Somebody made a recording of the performance the band gave a few nights before the festival in a local bar, and the recording confirmed that Mitch was right: Gypsy Sun and Rainbows did not play well together. Jimi was unfazed. He felt he could whip the band into shape.

Promoted as "An Aquarian Exposition: Three Days of Peace and Music," the fair became the most famous music festival in history, as we all know. And the "Woodstock" festival, as almost everybody also knows, was not held in Woodstock but in Bethel, yet to this day, everyone refers to it as Woodstock.

The company that organized the event, Woodstock Ventures, was founded by four semi-inexperienced and naive promoters: John Roberts, Joel Rosenman, Artie Kornfeld, and Michael Lang. They were trying to raise enough money to build a recording studio in Woodstock. With that in mind, they watched on August 15, 1969, as thousands of people gathered at a six-hundred-acre dairy farm for what would become one of the biggest events in music history.

The three days of "peace and music" that unfolded from August 15 to18 far exceeded anyone's expectations musically but not financially. Before the event, 186,000 tickets were sold—but the actual turnout was so high that the festival was opened up to the public for free once the concertgoers stormed the fences and tore them down. The festival, which featured thirty-two acts in total, was chaotic, rainy, muddy, festive, eventful, extraordinary, peaceful, and a once-in-a-life-time experience—and it forever changed the history of music.

Before they approached the townspeople of Woodstock to get their permission, in their arrogance the promoters decided it was a no-brainer and the concert would definitely be held in Woodstock. After all, why would Woodstock not want a concert named after itself? The town had a reputation for being a cultural mecca for artists and musicians.

In the early 1930s and '40s, Woodstock had been the home of the Byrdcliffe Artist Residency program, through which writers and artists came together to attend classes, and see concerts as well as theater events. This created Woodstock's artist colony reputation. In the 1960s it became a bohemian arts center, then people in the folk music and rock 'n' roll crowds heard about it and one by one started moving there, largely thanks to Albert Grossman. He managed many of the artists who moved there to be near him; others moved there because they wanted to be near him, hoping he would manage them.

By the time Michael Lang and his partners started organizing the talent for the festival, the town of Woodstock was already established as an arts-and-music colony. Bob Dylan lived there, as I mentioned. Also Van Morrison, Paul Butterfield, Janis Joplin, and Peter Yarrow of Peter, Paul and Mary, among many others. And, of course, Hendrix lived at the Shokan House and rehearsed his new band at the Tinker Street Cinema.

The promoters figured, "What could go wrong?" They assumed the village of Woodstock would welcome them and their festival with open arms. However, the town planners, despite Woodstock's reputation as a music-friendly community, turned down their proposal in early 1969. The main reason was the potential number of fans the festival likely would attract. The planners didn't want their town overrun with concertgoers. The promoters estimated that fifty thousand people would attend; we all know now they were wrong, and the town of Woodstock was right.

If you visit Woodstock today, as I have many times because I live in the vicinity, you would see that it's filled with souvenir shops and tie-dyed-clothing stores—which, in my opinion, have taken away from its former bohemian charm. Regardless, it's still a great community.

Turned down by Woodstock, the promoters decided to move the fair to Saugerties, which was ten miles from Woodstock and was where The Band lived at the infamous house known as "Big Pink." The promoters were turned down again for the same reason. It was now the spring of 1969, and the concert was planned for August. Desperate, the organizers traveled thirty-five miles south of Woodstock to Wallkill, New York. There they managed to rent three hundred acres in an industrial park, where they could hold the concert. They felt secure that they had their venue, and started creating posters and fliers for the event. Again, what could go wrong, right? They had paid the rent and had their venue. However, one month before the festival, on July 15, the town of Wallkill rescinded its permit for the festival on the grounds that the portable restrooms did not meet the Wallkill city code for an estimated crowd of fifty thousand people. The townspeople didn't want the festival in their community and forced the promoters out.

This must have freaked out the organizers—being rejected by three communities while they were in the process of printing tickets, posters, and promotional materials. And, worst of all, they already had major music acts signed that they would have to pay and wouldn't be able to if the festival didn't take place.

This was 1969, and the country was fighting a controversial war in Vietnam, a war that most young people vehemently opposed. It was also the era of the civil rights movement; Martin Luther King Jr. and Bobby Kennedy had been assassinated the year before. It was a time of many protests, much civil disobedience, and much political unrest. The organizers were promoting the festival as an opportunity for young people to escape into music and to spread the message of unity and peace. They had to find a place to put on the festival. They just had to.

I have no idea how they found the place to hold the festival and who did find it, but they must have panicked and scrambled to find a venue precisely one month before the actual concert was scheduled to take place. They did, in Bethel, a community of less than four thousand people in Sullivan County that was an hour and a half southwest of Woodstock. A dairy farmer named Max Yasgur rented them his six-hundred-acre field for a reported $50,000 (approximately $418,000 in today's dollars), which was more than what the three top performers were being paid combined, including Jimi. Since this was a private transaction with the landowner and not with the town of Bethel, they could go ahead with their festival. It would be confined to the privately owned farm and, as such, the town could not stop them.

The reason they didn't change the name of the festival from Woodstock to something else was because they had already started promoting the festival under the name of Woodstock, mistakenly believing that's where it was going to be held. All the talent had already been booked under the name Woodstock Ventures, and, as I mentioned, posters were already being printed. It was too late for the promoters to change the name to the Bethel Music Festival three weeks before the concert was going to take place. The name Woodstock stuck by default.

Woodstock went on to become a platform for the counterculture movement of the late 1960s through the 1970s. It made the country realize that young people had the power to alter the course of history. It legitimized young people's perspectives on civil rights, individual freedoms, and the Vietnam War. Woodstock has since come to represent a cultural phenomenon in the course of American history.

I was wrapped up in my own world when a few days before the festival, Jimi's office called, telling me to bring my cameras to the office, pick up a ticket, and get myself up to the festival to take pictures. They said Jimi wasn't planning to show up until the third and final day of the festival, and they wanted me there to cover his performance.

Because of my hesitation and the reluctance in my voice, Kathy got on the phone and, in her no-nonsense manner, said, "Grab your camera and get up there. We'll messenger the ticket down to you as soon as we get them."

"Look, Kathy, why me? I'm tired of running back and forth upstate."

Without missing a beat, she tore into me. "Jimi's photographer took off to London, and we need the event covered. You understand? Because I don't think you do. We need it covered! If you're so fucking good, prove it!"

She wasn't kidding. I gave in. I would have done anything to please Kathy, and I'm glad of that, because if I hadn't felt that way, I would never have gone. I would never have caved. Not to Bob Levine. Not to Mike Jeffery. Not even to Jimi. But I always said yes to Kathy. She also told me there was a surprise from Jimi waiting for me. Grudgingly, I agreed.

Three days later, on August 14, someone rang my bell. Through the intercom, I was told that there was a package for me downstairs. I lived in a five-flight walk-up apartment, so I had no desire to go downstairs and then back up.

"Bring it up," I told the delivery person.

"You have to sign for it," he said.

"Okay, fine, I'll sign for it, no big deal. Bring it up."

"It's too big. It wouldn't fit through the door."

"Are you kidding? What is it?"

The messenger was insistent. I wanted to be angry, but by now I was just too damn curious, so I went down the five flights of stairs.

Standing outside at the curb was the messenger, who was actually someone who worked in the office. He was standing next to a brand-new British Racing Green Fiat convertible.

"They told me to tell you this is from Jimi," he said. "You have to sign for it."

I was totally blown away.

He handed me the paperwork, which I had trouble reading because I was so stunned. In my wildest imagination, I would never have anticipated this happening. After I signed all the paperwork, he handed me one more page. By signing it, I agreed to leave for Bethel immediately with, of course, all three of my cameras. There were instructions attached on what to do when I got there. I knew the car wasn't a surprise from Jimi. I was sure he didn't even know about it. Sometime later I found out this was the case when I thanked him and he didn't even know what I was talking about. I learned it was Kathy who'd set the whole thing up. Well, her ploy worked.

I left within sixty minutes of getting my surprise. I ran back upstairs, taking two or three stairs at a time, grabbed my camera bag and cameras, took several rolls of film out of the fridge, and stuffed a backpack with several T-shirts, socks, a jacket, a towel, a toothbrush, toothpaste, and other necessities.

Once downstairs, I tossed everything in the trunk of the car, and then, still trying to process what had just happened, I drove off. At Twenty-Third Street and Eighth Avenue I stopped for a light. Standing on the corner about to cross the street was the most angelic-looking, cool, wide-eyed, beautiful hippie girl I had ever seen. At that moment I forgot all about Kathy. I couldn't take my eyes off her. She stopped in front of the car, paused, and looked directly at me. Then she smiled and casually said, "Nice car. Drive me uptown, even if you're not going uptown."

She walked around to the passenger door, opened it, smiled, and got in the car. I was too stunned to respond.

The light changed to green, and I had to move.

"I'm April," she said.

A few blocks up when I stopped for another light, I blurted out, "Listen, I need to get on the West Side Highway. I'm not going uptown; I'm going upstate to the Woodstock concert."

"Well then, so am I."

"I need to leave *right now*, and you don't have a toothbrush, a change of clothes, or anything. Nothing."

"Come on, there's going to be someplace up there where I can buy underwear and a toothbrush," she said.

How do you respond to that? You don't.

The light changed, and I drove off. April stood up in the front seat and shouted to the world, "We're going to *Woodstock*!"

I should have realized then that this was not going to end well.

With nothing but the clothes on her back, and me having only what I'd put in my backpack, I headed for Woodstock. I don't think we said two words to each other the entire way up. We just listened to the radio announcers talking about the festival and a constant stream of music by the artists scheduled to appear.

Jimi, I would learn later, stayed upstate at the Shokan House rehearsing his new band. Having played several festivals already, they didn't expect this one to be a big deal. What had helped influence Jimi's decision was that he would be the headlining act. Some of the band members thought the festival was going be a bust, and they voiced that to Jimi. On top of that, Mitch Mitchell found Jimi's new band to be nothing like The Experience. One week before the festival, Mitch remarked to Jonathan that this was the only band he had ever played in that had gotten worse, not better, with practice.

Upon hearing of the change of venue and knowing that Bethel was at least a good two hours from New York City, Michael Jeffery didn't expect very many fans to even bother making the drive. The promoters predicted that at least one hundred thousand tickets would be sold, but that wasn't the case. Only fifty thousand to sixty thousand advance tickets had been sold, and sales were leveling off.

I'd thought it would be a breeze driving up to Bethel but was soon confronted with reality: bad traffic on the New York State Thruway. A trip that should have taken ninety minutes took over four hours. So much for my getting there early. As I got closer, it became obvious that thousands of concertgoers had abandoned their cars on the side of the road and begun to walk. Looking at the license plates on several of the abandoned cars—Washington, California, Massachusetts, Ohio, New Jersey, Florida, Texas, and on and on—I knew this was not just another concert. I felt in my gut that it was going to be something big.

It made no sense to continue driving; it was becoming nearly impossible to drive on the narrow two-lane country road, because it was jammed with concertgoers walking to the festival. I finally parked on the side of a road about three miles from the concert site. A brand-new car with less than 250 miles on it, left at the side of the road. I hoped it would be there when I got back.

April and I started walking to the site carrying one back-pack plus three cameras and rolls of film. The swelling crowds along the way built a feeling of elation and created a party spirit. I had never experienced anything like it before—and still haven't since.

By now more than two hundred thousand fans were now descending on the concert site, and it was only Friday after-noon. Only about sixty thousand or so had tickets. I was one of them, but it didn't matter. People tore the fences down and streamed onto the hillsides of Yasgur's farm overlooking the concert stage. Soon the promoters were forced to declare that the Woodstock Music & Arts Fair was now free.

On that Friday, before the concert had even started, an estimated four thousand people took over the concert site, and more were on the way. It was becoming the biggest rock concert in human history.

After walking over the torn-down gates and onto the concert site, I found a spot on a hill looking down at the stage. The concert site with its stage was in a bowl-shaped cow pasture. I figured I might as well grab a good spot while I could, especially seeing all the out-of-state license plates that were already here, and knowing that more would be coming. April, in the meantime, charmed two stoned college guys into giving her a sleeping bag, a towel, and a blanket. They didn't have a toothbrush and definitely no women's underwear, but I was still impressed with what she managed to get. Then again, the entire vibe was one of unity, peace, enjoyment, and sharing.

After we got settled, I told April that I had to try to get backstage. By now she knew why I was there and why I had brought three cameras with me. I told her I didn't have a pass for her; in fact, I didn't even have a pass for myself, but I had some vague instructions, so I was going to give it a shot.

April looked at me and said, "If you want to fuck me, you're going to bring me backstage."

I tried to explain why that would be impossible if I didn't get myself back there first, and that taking her along would only complicate things. Then I flat-out refused. Well, so much for peace and love. She went off on me, and we got into an argument. I didn't have time to deal with this, nor did I want to, so I told her to stay on top of the hill and that I would be back for her as soon as I had taken care of everything, and that I probably would be able to bring her backstage with me then. That calmed her down. I walked away.

Jimi and the band were still at the Shokan House, sitting there watching reports on the single television in the living room. By now the New York State Thruway was shut down. The gang was blown away. Nobody had a clue what was happening.

On my way to the backstage gate, I made my way through a sea of people, feeling like a speck. Finally, I made it to the backstage entrance gate. Not surprisingly, there was a long line of people trying to get backstage. But the vibe throughout the concert grounds was really great—a kind of happy-time mayhem. While I was waiting in line for what seemed like forever to get backstage, the concert started. It was now around five p.m., and I could hear Richie Havens performing. He was the first performer at Woodstock, and he played for three hours. (Coincidentally, years later, when I was a television producer for The Family Channel, I hired Richie for a gospel television special. We became friends after that.)

When I finally got to the head of the line, which took an eternity, I noticed it was the only backstage entrance gate. It was more like a fenced doorway, and there was some serious security. I gave my name to a beefy guard, who looked about as wide as he was tall. He checked list A, then list B, and finally list C.

"You're not on the list," he announced.

"Please check again. I'm there," I insisted.

"I've heard that all day. You're not on any list, okay? Sorry. There's a whole bunch of phones way over there. Try calling." He pointed to a bank of phones surrounded by people trying to make a call. "Now move along."

I thought about it. It was now almost dark, and I still had tomorrow. Besides, Jimi wasn't scheduled to show up until Sunday, and it was only Friday, so I decided to go back up the hill to find April. I remember Arlo Guthrie came onstage and performed. There were others before him, but I don't remember who. Later I would learn that Guthrie started playing just before midnight. I had no idea; I had lost all sense of time. It seems everyone else had, too.

In the place where I had left April, a small pup tent was now pitched. All I could make out inside was a sleeping bag with a lot of motion going on. I think Joan Baez was now onstage. It started to drizzle, so I opened the tent flap—and found April naked with two guys in a sleeping bag.

She was wasted. Totally high. "Come on, Johnny baby, join the party," she said.

"No thanks. It looks like all the entrances are taken."

It started to rain, not very hard but steadily. I had to crawl into the tent whether I wanted to or not, so I wedged myself inside up against one wall of it. April was cavorting in the sleeping bag with someone. They were completely ignoring me, and the other guy was fast asleep. I passed out. I think I slept all night; I don't remember.

I have no idea how early it was when I woke up, and if I had even fully slept at all, but I crawled out of the tent. I was cold and wet. We all were. And we stayed that way for the next three days. I stood up and looked around, and all I saw was a sea of people—a mass of humanity all in one place, as Crosby, Stills, Nash & Young would later say. I should have known then this was going to be the musical event of the century.

The crowd had swelled to unbelievable proportions overnight. There was not one piece of vacant land. You couldn't even see a blade of grass, and this had been a cow pasture just a few days ago. People were everywhere. Partying. Sleeping. Smoking pot. Socializing. Laughing. Singing. I looked around me and at the small tent, and I knew that the tent wouldn't be standing much longer. People were encroaching on every inch of ground and pushing closer together.

Eventually, the crowd was almost shoulder to shoulder as far as I could see. It seemed like half the planet had showed up, and all of them appeared to be under the age of thirty. There were so many people in that cow pasture bowl that if you moved your arm or stood up, someone would stick their leg there, claim it, and your spot would be gone.

Despite this, there was no animosity. You could feel the vibe in the air. It was a feeling that I can't describe, and I won't even try. But there was rain. There had been showers overnight, and if my memory serves me correctly, it was drizzling again Saturday morning. Looking back, who could have known it would rain? There was no twenty-four-hour Weather Channel, and no one really paid much attention to the weather reports on the radio. Plus, it had been hot and sunny on Friday morning. It was August, and nobody thought the rest of the weekend would be any different. Bringing rain gear or ponchos was the furthest thing from anybody's mind.

Looking back, I can't believe that there was no such thing as bottled water back then. Walk through any market today and you get hit with over two dozen choices. Back then, there wasn't even one. I think the mindset of everyone at the festival was, "We'll get there and there will be water and food." Well, it didn't quite happen that way. It was miserable, and very uncomfortable, and yet everyone put up with it, and I have only fond memories of what went on. My situation wasn't that of your typical Woodstock concertgoer, but ask pretty much anyone today who was there, and they'll tell you it was one of the greatest experiences they ever had.

As I stood on the hill outside that tiny pup tent, looking down at the bowl toward backstage, I shifted my line of sight to the row of about thirty pay phones. Reaching them would be difficult, but I had to get a call through to the office and get a name that would let me get backstage. The pay phones were all lined up in a row about a quarter mile down the road on the festival grounds. I decided to go for it.

What should have taken about twenty minutes ended up taking over an hour. While the music played onstage—I think it was Country Joe McDonald—I made my way down the hill toward the phones, maneuvering around, stepping on, and often climbing over people who were stretched out as far as the eye could see. I must have taken a dozen hits from joints handed to me as I zigzagged between people, occasionally stopping to chat with a cool-looking girl or guy.

When I reached the phones, it wasn't much better. There was a line that stretched for what seemed to be forever. I had no idea how long I waited in line, inching closer to get to an open phone. Those that were on drugs never stopped talking once they managed to get to a phone, because they no longer had any sense of time and space. There were no cell phones, so I had no choice but to wait. I wanted to get backstage to do what I had come there to do: shoot pictures.

Finally a phone freed up, and I grabbed it. Even though it was a Saturday, miraculously I managed to get through to Kathy at the office. Thank God. I had to shout into the phone to be heard. "How am going to take pictures of Jimi if I can't get onstage!" I shouted to Kathy. I explained the situation, and she gave me several names of people to ask for at the backstage entrance.

Because I had to shout into the phone to be heard, everyone near me could hear me too, and picked up on the name Jimi Hendrix when I shouted it. When I hung up, a trail of stoners followed me, and I realized they were going to follow me all the way to the backstage security gate. So I turned and headed back up the hill, weaving in and out of concertgoers until those that were following realized I wasn't going to the backstage entrance, and one by one dropped off. When the last one did, I turned around and made my way back down to the backstage entrance, which took another twenty minutes.

I encountered the same beefy security guard, but this time he recognized the name I gave him. He told me to wait, then came back and let me through. I felt as if I had entered paradise. I could breathe.

I asked every security guard I could find, "Hey, where's Hendrix's trailer?" I would point at my camera bag and add,

"I'm here to take pictures for him." No one knew. They weren't even sure there was a trailer yet, because he wasn't scheduled to show up until the following afternoon. Then I saw Paul Butterfield and went up to him. I asked him about Jimi, but he didn't know a thing. The rain was coming, we both knew, so he took me to his trailer, introduced me to his band members who were there, and told them I was welcome to use the Paul Butterfield Blues Band trailer. If he hadn't done that, I don't know what I would have done. At least I now had some type of base of operations backstage, and a place to keep my cameras safe as I went back and forth between the stage and the camera pit they had set up below the front of the stage. When I finally sat down in a chair, I just crashed. When I woke up, around two thirty p.m., I could hear Santana performing. Nobody knew who Santana was back then, and I was no different, but what I was hearing was mind-boggling. I had to see who was creating this amazing sound.

Santana was the surprise hit of Woodstock—a psychedelic jam band from San Francisco that blended Latin and African polyrhythms into blues-rock. I believe they were the first band to mix congas with guitars. They hadn't even released their first album yet. They were virtually unknown when they took the stage, and forty-five minutes later that all had changed. It became known that the only reason Santana had been invited to perform was because their manager was Bill Graham, who was probably the most powerful concert promoter in the United States. He forced the Woodstock promoters to book Santana. In reviews and articles on Woodstock during the weeks that followed, Santana was highlighted as the breakout band at Woodstock. They nailed it. It put them on the map. Within days of their performance, Santana's debut album was released. Word spread about their performance at Woodstock, and the album rose to number four on the U.S. *Billboard* chart, and their single "Evil Ways" landed in the top ten. Santana's appearance has always been regarded as one of the highlights of the festival.

I walked up the hill, sinking in mud, to a soundtrack provided by Santana. It was truly surreal. It took me forever to make my way up the hill, not only because of the mass of humanity I needed to climb over but because I would keep stopping to turn around and watch Santana perform. Amazingly, each member of the band was given the opportunity to do his own solo. It was almost like they were playing tribal rhythms. At one point it seemed like all five hundred thousand concertgoers got on their feet and were dancing, shouting, clapping, and becoming part of the music. The band member I remember the best, the one who really blew the audience away, was the drummer. Word was that he was only seventeen years old. His drum solo probably was the most memorable drum solo of the whole festival. We all were clapping our hands above our heads and shouting, "More, more, more, more," as the band walked offstage. I think they were so energized by the sheer magnitude of the reception they were getting that Carlos Santana turned around, and the rest of the band followed him. They returned to the stage to play an encore for an amazed and captivated audience.

Being that it was August, it was really hot. It was ninety-two degrees, and the humidity was 97 percent. The entire arena turned into a sauna, and the rain didn't help. The field became a mud pit. The amazing thing is, nobody seemed to care. When I got up to the tent site, April was gone. The tent was gone, too, and about a half dozen people were huddled together on one blanket, digging the music, having a great time, loving it, stoned. That image is still in my mind. So I joined them. That was so Woodstock.

A lot of heavy hitters performed on Saturday, including The Grateful Dead, Jefferson Airplane, Janis Joplin, Creedence Clearwater Revival, and The Who. The lighting designer introduced each group. His name was Chip Monck. He had been pressed into service by one of the promoters, and he, by default, became the emcee for the festival, making all the announcements. We all got to know his name and his voice, and we actually looked forward to his running commentary between acts as to what was happening on the concert grounds. He issued warnings like, "Don't eat the brown acid," explained the helicopters hovering overhead, let us know when the rains were coming, and kept us updated on the locations of first-aid tents and free commune food, plus he made at least a dozen other announcements.

He truly became the voice of the festival, even though he had never done this before. This guy was a lighting designer, for God's sake. He had designed the lighting rig at the Monterey Pop Festival, and for shows by The Rolling Stones and The Byrds at the Hollywood Bowl. I would later find out at Jimi's office the following week that Chip was paid $7,000 for ten weeks' worth of work to get the Woodstock lighting rigs up and running at the first venue. Then the venue kept changing, and when the promoters finally settled on Bethel, there was nobody around to introduce the artists onstage—the person had quit—so an inexperienced "announcer" was pulled off the lighting rigs and pressed into service. It could have been anybody. By fate, it was him. The perfect choice. Who would have thought?

He even kept us updated on Wavy Gravy, who was the head of a food co-op called the Hog Farm. Thank God for the Hog Farm, because after a while, it was the only source of food, even if most of the time it was cold mush. The people from Hog Farm were the unsung heroes of the festival, dealing with every issue that came up—delays, injuries, the rain, the mud, food provisions, and clean drinking water. In a way, they probably were responsible for helping to keep the show running.

Up on the hill, I fell asleep between two girls and some guy, all of us on the ground covered by whatever we could find to shelter us from the rain. I must have been really wasted, because when I woke up, I think it was five thirty in the morning. The Who was playing onstage. I watched the rest of their performance and witnessed the famous incident in which the activist Abbie Hoffman jumped onstage condemning the concert when another activist John Sinclair was "rotting in jail." That was about all he could say before Pete Townshend swung his guitar around and knocked Hoffman off the stage, without missing a note. It was a priceless moment.

It was Sunday, day three. Jimi and his band were scheduled to close the show that night, so I knew he would be arriving today—or so I thought. Right now, like everyone else, I had a set of issues to deal with that came with a poorly planned and ill-equipped event. The porta-potties were overflowing. Concertgoers were using the cornfields as bathrooms. There were emergency medical announcements being made that couldn't be dealt with because the roads leading to the festivals were blocked and ambulances could not get through. Helicopters were brought in to airlift the really bad cases out to a hospital. I heard there was a helicopter on twenty-four-hour standby at Grossinger's, a popular family resort nearby in the Catskill Mountains, that could get to the festival site within ten minutes—and did, to handle a victim of alcohol poisoning. It went on like that almost nonstop.

The festival site was declared a disaster area, and Sullivan County had declared a state of emergency. New York governor Nelson Rockefeller was so alarmed by the crowds that he planned to send the military in, but one of the organizers, John Roberts, talked him out of it. Those of us who were there had no idea we were in a state of emergency; we were having one big, fantastic party. It was a love fest. And the music was fantastic.

The concert did not resume until Sunday afternoon at two p.m., with Joe Cocker as the first act. Joe Cocker was a Brit who had been in the music business for quite a while, but the Woodstock audience hardly knew him. I had no idea who he was. When he started singing and revealed a soulful Ray Charles–like voice, he became famous; it was probably the best performance of his career. To this day, I feel that his version of "With a Little Help From My Friends" is the best that's ever been performed or recorded. It was a triumph.

As soon as the song ended, a heavy thunderstorm came out of nowhere and shut everything down. You could see it coming. The huge storm barreled towards the festival grounds, and the stage crew frantically covered the stage with tarps. The storm washed over the festival, and everything was brought to a halt for several hours. Thousands of concertgoers took off to the makeshift vendor booths in the woods, known as Bindy's Bazaar for shelter. There just wasn't enough shelter.

I managed to get backstage and climb the steps to the stage partway up to see what was happening. Not a very smart move, given what was happening. I could see the concert field, and it was unbelievable: waves and waves of torrential rain pouring down on thousands of people who had nowhere to go. There were untold numbers in groups of six, eight, even ten, huddled under green tarps trying to stay dry. Others were covering themselves with sleeping bags, which were completely useless, because they soaked up the rainwater like a sponge. Those that could not find shelter ended up playing in the mud, which was everywhere. The whole cow pasture became a giant mud pit. The image is burned into my brain, but I can't even come close to describing it properly.

Rather than be yanked down from my position and thrown out of the backstage area, I got down as quickly as I could and, like a drowned rat, started making my way to the Butterfield Blues Band trailer. That's when I heard an announcer shouting into the microphone for everyone to get away from the light and sound towers, and warning those who were sitting on the towers that they could be electrocuted. Then in the middle of that, he changed his tone and told the people in the crowd that if they were to think really hard, maybe they could stop the rain! A chant of "No rain, no rain, no rain" started in the crowd and built up. I even got caught up in it, along with some stagehands backstage. At the time, I didn't realize how naive we all were. In the torrential rain, the stage was sliding in the mud, but the fans were unfazed. They were dancing and singing in the rain and playing in the mud, which to this day is part of the iconic imagery associated with Woodstock. We were young, and we believed we could change the world...and in some way, we did.

The storm threw the entire schedule off and set the performance times back several hours for all the performers, including Jimi, who was scheduled to close the festival at eleven p.m. that night (Sunday). I heard that he was still at the Shokan House with his band, because the rainstorm was affecting everything. I would later learn that the concert promoters contacted the house and told the band that they had arranged for a large military helicopter to fly them and their instruments down to the concert site. It had stopped raining by the time Jimi and his band left the house, and they all went to the local airport, which really wasn't much of an airport at all. By the time they got to the airport it was raining again, and they learned that the concert site had been turned into one huge mud bath, even backstage.

The storm blew through in twenty minutes, but it was pretty intense. The stage, which had slid six inches downhill, was restrained by the stage crew so the show could continue. Mel Lawrence and Michael Lang asked Max Yasgur, the farmer who owned the land all five hundred thousand of us were on, to say a few words to the crowd. With encouragement from Lawrence and Lang, Chip Monck introduced Yasgur to the crowd, saying, "This is the man whose farm we're on—Mr. Max Yasgur." The crowd went wild, absolutely wild. Being close enough to the stage, I could see that Yasgur was blown away by the sea of people before him.

He stepped up to the microphone, and even though I don't remember everything he said, I do remember his opening statement: "I'm a farmer. I don't know how to speak to twenty people at one time, let alone a crowd like this." He went on to say that this was the largest group of people ever assembled in one place for a concert event, and that we all had proved something to the world: that half a million kids can get together and have three days of fun and music and have *nothing* but fun and music. The crowd went nuts. They loved him! Shortly afterward, the music started again. I don't remember which performer, because I went backstage again.

As I mentioned, Jimi was scheduled to arrive on the last day of the festival, Sunday, but now it was Sunday and the fields were sticky with cold mud and there was almost no food. The festival was falling apart and far behind schedule because of the rain and the power failures. You could see people leaving; as great as it was, they'd had enough. A trip to the porta-potties took an hour each way. The official food vendors had run out of supplies the very first night, and the concert was into the third night. The only food was macrobiotic dishes being served up by volunteers from the Hog Farm collective. Out of the five hundred thousand original concertgoers, only about 180,000 were left—at least that was the number being thrown around backstage on Sunday night. I firmly believed that most of the remaining fans were waiting for Jimi.

I don't know how Jimi got there, but I would hear a story a week later in New York City back at the office. One of the office assistants said that there was no military helicopter waiting at the local airport, because when Jimi and the band arrived, it was pouring rain and too dangerous to fly. No flights were taking off. At the small airport, the group came upon Crosby, Stills, Nash & Young, who were also trying to get to the concert site. Out of desperation, one of the band members allegedly stole a truck, and they all piled in and drove down to Bethel, a little over an hour south of the local airport. It seems a little farfetched to me, but it made for a good story. Sometime later, Neil Young would say that stealing a truck with Jimi Hendrix was one of the high points of his life—better even than the actual Woodstock concert.

Anyway, at this point on Sunday night, the show was almost ten hours behind and was now approaching day four. The only explanation I can give as to what was holding it all together was the "peace and love and music" vibe. Technical and weather delays caused the festival to stretch into Monday morning. The organizers gave Jimi the opportunity to go on at midnight of day three, but he turned them down, wanting to close the show.

By now I was wearing out my welcome in the Butterfield trailer, so no matter how tired I was, I spent most of my time out of it, mostly in the photographer's pit in front of the stage. It wasn't very comfortable, being that it was filled with movie camera men, film equipment, still photographers, and probably a lot of people who didn't belong there.

I managed to catch an amazing set by Ten Years After, one of my favorite bands. Alvin Lee was an extraordinary guitar player. Struggling to stay awake, I tried to catch Crosby, Stills, Nash & Young and did catch most of it. Then the Paul Butterfield Blues Band came on at six a.m. on Monday. I felt I owed it to them to stay awake. When they finished, I made my way out of the pit and, with my two remaining cameras (I have no idea what happened to the third one) and only a couple of rolls of film left, I went up onstage to get a feel for the layout. Onstage, I could see that the audience had dwindled considerably. I would read later that there were only about thirty thousand die-hard concertgoers remaining. It sure looked like it.

I was onstage with my cameras trying to figure out the best focal points to get the shots I wanted. When I turned around to leave, since there was one final act before Jimi went on, I ran smack into Mike Jeffery. He was standing right behind me.

"Where you going?" He wasn't being confrontational; it was a genuine question.

"Uh, I, ah, I was...I was going to come back when Jimi went on."

"No. No. You can't. You have to see this next band. You have to."

Jeffery was very excited, almost childlike. He was almost pleading with me to stay and watch the next band.

"You've never seen anything like them," he said. "They are throwbacks. They're so old, they're new. You've got to see them. They're a new band. Jimi found them. Stay. Stay." I knew then that was exactly what I was going to do.

The band was Sha Na Na. They were a fledgling band and were getting to play Woodstock only because Jimi had heard them play in New York at The Scene and convinced the Wood-stock promoters to book them. It was a career-launching moment for them, and it wouldn't have happened if it weren't for Jimi. This originally unknown a cappella group of Colum-bia University greasers had secured the prime slot, just before Jimi's festival-closing set.

I have to say, Sha Na Na was unique and probably the coolest act to play Woodstock, and their set wouldn't have happened if Jimi and, yes, Mike Jeffery, hadn't enthusiastically embraced them. They got a thirty-minute set, and I remember that they were totally bonkers. Their set was so theatrical that it was practically performance art. They got what amounted to a standing ovation from those audience members that were still able to stand after such an extraordinary weekend. Sha Na Na became known as "the band that was born at Woodstock." They were considered the most out-of-place band there, but the audience thought they were great. Jeffery stood next to me for the entire performance. He loved every minute of it. So did I. As the band walked off the stage, Jeffery mentioned he had to go, and Jimi was about to come on.

Then he turned and said, "No hard feelings about our meeting, right? I hope you don't hold grudges, but keep in mind what we talked about." Then he warmly shook my hand, laughed, and left, leaving me dumbfounded. At that point I was sure the man was schizoid or a psycho. Maybe both.

9

Jimi Hendrix Plays Woodstock

Gypsy Sun and Rainbows took the stage around eight thirty a.m. on Monday and were the last act to perform. The sun was out, finally, and it was burning away a lot of the moisture in the air. The announcer introduced the band as The Jimi Hendrix Experience. Jimi stepped up to the microphone and corrected him, telling the audience that they were Gypsy Sun and Rainbows.

Gypsy Sun and Rainbows was the largest band Jimi had ever played with—and the Blackest. The Jimi Hendrix Experience had been dominated by white musicians from England, but Gypsy Sun and Rainbows showcased Black musicians: Billy Cox, guitarist Larry Lee, the percussionist Juma Sultan, and, of course, Jimi. Also, it was the only Hendrix band that included a second guitarist, Larry Lee. Lee backed up Jimi on several songs and played some lead on a few numbers. He even sang lead on two songs. Strangely, there is virtually no footage of his solo guitar work that has ever been made public—or that I know of anyway.

By the time they took the stage, half the crowd had started their journey home, but it didn't faze Jimi. The band meandered at first, but to Jimi's credit as a band leader, he got them on track. He went on to play the longest set of his career: twenty-seven songs over two hours. Exhausted from shooting pictures of the festival during the previous three days, I couldn't even tell you the order of the songs or what they were. I was too busy maneuvering all over the stage, the photographer's pit, behind the stage, on the side of the stage. I was shooting pictures carefully, because by now I had limited amount of film left. I am honored that the book recently released by Janie Hendrix, Jimi's sister, honoring what would have been Jimi's eightieth birthday, included several pictures I took of him at Woodstock.

When I heard the opening bars of "Voodoo Child," I stopped for a bit to enjoy it. I think Jimi found his comfort spot with Voodoo Child, and he did one of the best versions I think he ever played of that song. But he didn't stop there; he continued with a medley lasting over half an hour, and then totally unexpectedly—probably even to his band members' surprise, because they stopped playing and listened as well—Jimi started playing the National Anthem. He performed it solo but not on its own. It was part of the medley that included hits like "Voodoo Child" as an unaccompanied improvisation lasting nearly five minutes.

That National Anthem solo would become symbolic not only of Woodstock but of the 1960s. With that performance, Jimi crystallized his legend forever. I didn't take one picture. I was in a hypnotic state. Nobody, and I mean nobody, expected "The Star-Spangled Banner" from the likes of Jimi Hendrix.

Looking out at the crowd, I could see a lot of the kids scratching their heads and rubbing sleep from their eyes. It was as if they could not believe what they were hearing. I doubt many of them were even aware that Jimi owned a rendition of this song.

But as the sun continued to rise and the crowd began to realize how special the performance was, Jimi was able to energize a tired, hungry, exhausted audience. He then roared through the most incredible version of "Purple Haze" I'd ever heard. It may have been the best performance I ever saw of his. When he finished his two-hour set and was leaving the stage, he did something he had never done before—and never did again. He did an encore. He closed the festival with his well-known cover of "Hey Joe." As the last notes faded out over the hungry, wasted, mud-crusted crowd of about twenty-five thousand, Woodstock became history.

Jimi's rendition of "The Star-Spangled Banner" and his performance came to define the Woodstock concert. The *New York Times* commented that it was the most electrifying moment of Woodstock and called it the single greatest moment of the '60s. Jimi had taken one of the best-known songs in American history and made it his own. When most people think of Jimi Hendrix and Woodstock, Jimi's three-minute-and-forty-six-second iconic performance of the National Anthem is what comes to mind.

Woodstock was the first, and only, time I was ever onstage during a Jimi Hendrix concert. When Jimi walked offstage, I followed shortly afterward. I should have been wasted—everyone should have been—but Jimi energized us with a bolt of energy even though we all had been in a zombie-like state. It was inexplicable and magical.

I went backstage to Butterfield's trailer to get my stuff. As I was standing in the doorway to leave, I saw Albert Grossman, Bob Dylan's manager, walking beside Jimi. In the middle of their conversation, a drugged-out guy with muddy clothes and filthy hair down to the middle of his back came over and shouted at Jimi, "Music should be free, man! It belongs to the people. You should be giving your money to the causes!"

Grossman ignored him and tried to pull Jimi along with him. But Jimi answered, "No, man, what we did here is beautiful. It's all positive. We're changing the world with music."

Grossman waved his arm in the direction of two men in his entourage, and they walked over to the stoned concertgoer. Each grabbed an arm and led him away as he shouted, "Fuck you! Free music for the world!" At that point Jimi also ignored him and walked off with Grossman.

I went back up to the top of the hill to find April, not expecting her to be there. But there she was, sitting on a mud-caked sleeping bag and looking like she hadn't slept or bathed for days—dirty hair dangling, mud covering her feet and hands, face smudged with dirt. She saw me and, without a word, got up and followed me down the hill and out to the road to the car. Hundreds of wasted concertgoers were all around us, all walking in the same direction. It was a soggy, dank, dreary parade of surprisingly jubilant concertgoers wandering to their cars or some other mode of transportation home. I had no hope of finding the car where we left it, but there it was. We got in and started our ride back to Manhattan.

During the entire drive back, neither of us spoke. We just listened to the radio, which was nonstop news about the Woodstock festival. One DJ came on and said that it had made history. He didn't have to tell us. We had been there; we knew it. He informed his listeners that during the festival there had been two births, two deaths, and more than four hundred people seeking medical attention for bad acid trips and other drug-related problems, but that everyone who had been there had witnessed some fantastic performances. Then he played "Purple Haze."

It seemed incredible, considering the number of people attending the festival (reportedly half a million), that only two people were officially reported as having died there. One was an eighteen-year-old who had been due to head off to Vietnam. His death is often attributed to a drug overdose, but later a *Time* magazine investigation showed that he could have had a heart problem brought on by hyperthermia. The other death was a seventeen-year-old who had been run over in his sleeping bag by a tractor collecting rubbish.

After the song on the radio ended, the DJ played a recording of John Sebastian announcing from the stage during his performance, "Some cat had a baby, and it's going to be far out!" Then the DJ played "Summer in the City," a Loving Spoonful song.

Although the DJ said two babies had been born at Woodstock, nobody's really sure. But the New York State Department of Health claimed there were over five thousand medical cases during the festival. The most common problem, according to Dr. William Abruzzi, who oversaw the medics, was not drugs, as is commonly believed. It was foot injuries suffered by concertgoers who took their wet shoes off.

A filmed Woodstock documentary was released in May 1970 and won the Academy Award for Best Documentary Feature. There was a soundtrack album from it as well. Years later it became known that the hippie couple on the album cover and the film's poster, Nick and Bobbi Ercoline, were amazingly still together. They had just started going out when they went to Woodstock, and a photographer snapped a picture of them wrapped in a blanket. According to ABC7, they married in 1971 and had two children. They were married for fifty-four years, until Bobbi died in March 2023.[*]

Not many couples today even come close to being together that long. It's inspiring.

* Emily Hartmann, "Bobbi Ercoline, woman shown hugging boyfriend on iconic Woodstock album, dies at 73," ABC7, March 29, 2023, https://abc7ny.com/woodstock-bobbi-ercoline-obituary-music-festival-new-york/13042308/.

10

Post-Peace and Love

A week or so after Woodstock, I don't quite remember exactly when, I decided to go back up to the Shokan House just to get away. I knew Jimi still had the house through the end of August. When I pulled into the driveway, I was surprised to see his white Corvette parked there. And I was glad because it was the only car there, so I knew he was alone. As I had done many times before, I knocked and then just walked in. I called out his name, but there was no response, so I just started wandering around the house. I eventually found him sitting alone out on the patio. He didn't look happy; I could tell something was bothering him.

I sat down and tried to engage him in a discussion about picking up the script again, but he didn't respond to that. Instead, he told me that the Black Panthers were really on his case, pressuring him to do a benefit concert to bail out twenty-one Panthers sitting in jail, accused of conspiring to bomb places in New York City. Jimi was willing to do the show but didn't want to be linked to the movement's reputation for vio-lence and radical thinking. He was clearly conflicted.

Jimi said, "I believe that the Black Power movement has things to say that people need to hear, but they're not really what I'm all about." Avoiding confrontation—typical for him—he added, "I left the decision to management."

He got up and disappeared into another part of the house. I knew enough not to follow him, so I just hung around outside.

Eventually, after I couldn't stand the August heat and hu-midity anymore, I went back into the house and found Jimi in the living room, quietly strumming an acoustic guitar. A little while later, a black limo pulled up into the driveway, stopped, and parked. Jimi asked me to go check it out. When I got outside, I found myself facing four men in black suits, looking like they had stepped right off the pages of *The Godfather*. They were not friendly. They ordered me to stay outside with the limo driver, who I was sure was one of them. He was dressed the same and clearly had some sort of position in their hierarchy. They barged through the front door.

I have no idea how long I waited aside, spending most of the time pacing back and forth on the patio after a failed attempt to try to make small talk with the driver. At one point one of the men appeared at the front door, half his body stick-ing out. He motioned to the driver, then went back inside. The driver then went toward a tree on the lawn, took out a gun, and, ignoring me as though I wasn't even there, fired two shots into the tree. He casually put the gun back into a side holster, then walked to the limo, leaned up against it, and waited.

I tried to act as if I wasn't fazed a bit, but it didn't matter, because he continued to act as if I wasn't there. Several minutes later the others emerged from the house and, without saying a word, got into the car and left. I waited until they were completely out of sight before I turned to go back into the house. No sooner had I started toward the front door than Jimi came out of the house. Without saying a word, he walked right past me, got into his car, and left. I drove off as well. It was the last time I was ever at the Shokan House.

Later that week, I stopped in at the New York office. There I met up with Jimi on the lower level, where I'd first met him. He seemed remarkably calm. I was still trying to process what had happened, so I flat out asked him. Jimi said the limo visit had been arranged by Jeffery. That's when I learned that certain bands that Jeffery managed or arranged bookings for were actually mob-controlled, and the mob had "requested" him to semi-manage them. In his slow, soft-spoken way, but clearly upset, Jimi told me that they had been there to deliver a message: that he should seriously reconsider ever changing management. They told him not to leave rock 'n' roll, and not to change his music or his musical style. They also remarked on his having a band predominantly of Black musicians. Jimi knew that had come straight from Jeffery. They told him to regroup The Jimi Hendrix Experience and go out on tour.

"The Jimi Hendrix Experience must tour and keep making money," Jimi told me. "They want me stuck."

I told him about Jeffery's behavior onstage during the concert. I wondered out loud if Jeffery had been in such a good mood because he had already set up the mob guys' visit.

Jimi said he didn't care about any of it, adding defiantly, "I'm going to go ahead and do whatever the fuck I want to do anyway."

I had the feeling that Jimi was going to do exactly what Jeffery wanted him to do. I hoped I was wrong.

Jimi didn't seem like he was interested in doing any more work on the script, so I stopped going to the office and mostly hung out with friends and did my best to continue writing on my own. One day I got a call from the office asking me to come down because Bob Levine wanted to talk to me. I went to the office and met with him. He was interested in trying to leverage *Avril* and asked me to explain the film's concept to Soft Machine, a rock band managed by Mike Jeffery. I agreed, and he arranged a meeting for that week. On the way out, he gave me a copy of the new Soft Machine album to familiarize myself with their music.

When we met, the band members liked the film's concept. No dialogue, spectacular color visuals, music solely setting the mood and acting as the dialogue while creating the emotional tone of what was happening on-screen. After they left, I thought it had been a good, productive meeting until Levine called me into his office and reamed me out. He told me that I had been "talking down" to the band members, some of whom had gone to Harvard.

"I wasn't talking down to them," I told him. "I was explaining the concept in the most basic terms, no different than I've explained it to others. It was more for me than it was for them."

"Bullshit! You were in the next goddamn office. The door was open. I heard it all."

At that moment his phone rang, and he took the call. Soon he was engrossed, arguing with someone on the other end. I just stood there. At that moment Kathy drifted in, undoubtedly having overheard what Bob had said to me. She slowly walked over to me and, while Bob was on the phone only a few feet away from us, ran her fingertip sensuously down the side of my cheek. I froze. I was very, very uncomfortable. I was thinking, *What is this all about?* Fortunately, Bob was so involved in his call that he didn't even notice. Kathy then brushed my hair aside, turned, and walked out. I left as quickly as I could without letting Bob know what had happened.

It was several days before I went back to the office. I wasn't thrilled about it but had to, because I had a meeting set up with Jimi to try one last time to get him to refocus on the script. The work was not going well at all.

I finally got to sit down with him in the basement apartment, which was becoming more like a sanctuary in the office where Jimi could disappear when he needed to. I told him about my meeting with Soft Machine, and he was not happy about it. He was emphatic that no one was going to dictate to him what music to use in the movie. He went on to tell me how much he liked Bob Levine and that "Bob is a good person, but many times Levine is only doing what Jeffery wants him to do."

I wasn't quite sure if that was the case. I had the feeling that Jeffery wasn't thrilled with Jimi's taking time to get involved with a spec script, so why would Bob reach out and help?

As we were talking, Kathy entered the room. She smiled at both of us and proceeded to tell Jimi that Jeffery said no to doing the Black Panthers benefit. She said that Jeffery felt that if Jimi were to become associated with such a dangerous, unpredictable movement, the government would have to start watching Jimi, which would then lead to the same repression that other radicals were experiencing.

"I figured the decision would come down that way, 'cause Jeffery hates me doing anything for free," Jimi said.

Jimi, however, did want to do something to show support for the Black community. Kathy suggested that he work with the Aleem twins, Taharqua and Tunde-Ra, his friends from his early days in Harlem, to put together a free street concert. It turned out that Jimi had already intended to do just that.

The Aleem twins were originally Albert and Arthur, but somewhere along the line, they changed their names. They were musicians, record producers, authors, and entrepreneurs based uptown in Harlem. Many years later, in the 1980s, they would found an independent record label, NIA Records, which would have some club/dance hits. They would be instrumental in kick-starting the careers of several well-known hip-hop artists, including Marley Marl and Wu-Tang Clan. However, before any of this happened, as struggling musicians living in Harlem, they met another struggling musician named Jimi Hendrix through a couple of mutual girlfriends, and they all ended up sharing an apartment in the West Village for almost two years.

Jimi always went back to them, because they had befriended him before he went to London, when he was still a nobody. Jimi always made sure that he stayed connected to them. The three of them even became musical collaborators, and Jimi gave them their stage name, the Ghetto Fighters. Little-known fact: They did backup vocals on eight of Jimi's albums, including for the songs "Freedom," "Stepping Stone," "Dolly Dagger," and "Izabella." And Jimi even would end up playing guitar on one of their recordings for a song called "Mojo Man," overdubbed at Electric Lady Studios in August 1970—one month before he died. I only met them once, in passing. I didn't really know who they were. I would learn a lot more about them from Jimi later when he would tell me that he was planning to produce a Ghetto Fighters album—a "street opera."

Tundre Ra Aleem died in 2014, but before he did, he and his brother influenced virtually every musical genre of that era. They were responsible for some great rock, blues, R&B, rap, and dance music recorded at the time. And as I said, Jimi decided to connect with them to produce and promote a Harlem concert, to show the Black Panthers he wanted to give back.

11

Harlem Street Concert

The original plan was for Jimi to do a benefit concert for the humanitarian crisis in Nigeria (known as Biafra at the time) held at the famous Harlem concert venue the Apollo Theater. However, the Jewish owners of the Apollo, the Schiffman family, turned them down, so they decided to take it outdoors. Jimi would give a free benefit concert for the United Block Association on a street corner in Harlem: Lenox Avenue and 139th Street. He and the Aleem brothers selected September 5, 1969, as the date for the concert. Interesting fact concerning the Apollo, Buddy Holly and The Crickets were the first white act to play the Apollo. The crowd booed them when they first came on because the audience thought they were going to see an R&B group, The Crickets. However, by the third night Buddy Holly had won them over.

Before the concert took place, Jimi made the announcement at a televised press conference at Frank's, a landmark restaurant on 125th Street that was Harlem's main meeting place for both Black and white businessmen. I was there, and most of the reporters weren't that interested in the United Block Association concert. They were constantly asking Jimi questions about his legendary performance at Woodstock about three weeks earlier. Jimi tried to keep the press conference focused on the concert, but the questions kept coming back to Woodstock and his performance there.

Afterward, Jimi and I and a few of his friends, and a couple of groupies, had drinks at a bar. Jimi told us that he was worried about playing rock 'n' roll, his music, for the uptown Black community.

"They're a tough crowd," he said. "They like what they know and not too much else. If they decide you sound white, you're dead."

At one point Jimi let it be known that Mike Jeffery wasn't too happy about the street concert. No surprise there. Jeffery also was not pleased that Jimi had yet to put The Experience back together and wasn't out touring, making money. And he was freaked out that Jimi suddenly had a big money problem. A decision had come down in a lawsuit over a 1965 contract that Jimi made with the record producer Ed Chalpin. (Coincidentally, I would meet Chalpin years later while working for a major home video distribution company.) The court had given Jimi a hard deadline to deliver a new album to Chalpin to cover the cost of the settlement. You could tell it was troubling him.

"I don't deliver, I get sued for five million dollars," Jimi told us.

On September 5, 1969, Jimi played the benefit on a stage the size of a closet. It was an all-day event, and Jimi, as usual, was set to go on last. The benefit concert was supported by artists on "Fat" Jack Taylor's Rojac Records, including Big

Maybelle, Chuck-a-Luck, and L.T.D. I took a subway up and got there just as Jimi pulled his white Corvette into a parking space. No sooner had he parked than a young guy snatched his guitar out of the back seat and took off. The Aleem twins knew people on the block, and they got the guitar back shortly. I have no idea how, or what happened to the kid who'd grabbed it, nor did I want to know. Then out of nowhere, Jimi's girlfriend Carmen showed up, and Jimi started getting flak from the promoters for having a blonde Puerto Rican girlfriend. I was beginning to question what I was doing there.

Finally, Jimi was about to go on, last. I watched the biggest blunder happen: The first band member onstage to set up was the white British drummer, Mitch Mitchell. Comments flew from the audience, like: "Get your cracker whitey ass back to Long Island!" People started to leave, so Billy Cox, Jerry Velez, Juma, and Larry Lee—Jimi's Woodstock band, Gypsy Sun and Rainbows, a mostly Black band—quickly got onstage. Seeing this, some of the audience members returned, but many didn't. At that point I didn't want to stay for the concert. I decided to let the music start, and then I could disappear unnoticed.

I would later find out that the concert had been set to be filmed professionally, but the person who had been paid to film it didn't realize how big a star Jimi was and ran out of film because he used it all filming the other acts. All that remains of that historic night is a few seconds of film of Jimi plugging into his amps, and some pictures taken by some professional photographers. There also is a horribly distorted audio recording that's barely audible, because the engineers were not experienced pros.

When Jimi's act started, the Harlem audience was not warmed up to him. Some people threw objects onstage. Jimi ignored it and got into his performance. Even though much of the audience left at that point, including me, I would later learn that he won over the remaining crowd and put on a great show. He debuted with "Machine Gun," and that went over really well. The fact that the lyrics are about the disproportionate number of Black soldiers getting sent to the front lines in Vietnam helped a lot. On my way out to the subway station, I noticed that Jimi's car had a parking ticket. I couldn't believe it. A NYPD cop had given Jimi Hendrix, the star of the show— which was a benefit concert he was doing for free, no less—a parking ticket! I thought it was lucky, at least, that the white Corvette Stingray convertible, which you couldn't miss, was still there.

12

The Dick Cavett Show

Jimi was booked on *The Dick Cavett Show* after the Harlem benefit concert. The office staff made arrangements to watch it on the office TV, but I watched it sitting in my apartment. The show was on in the afternoon; it hadn't yet moved to late night. It was hosted by Dick Cavett (naturally) and ran on ABC-TV from 1968 to 1975, opposite NBC's *The Tonight Show Starring Johnny Carson.*

Cavett was such a skillful host that he could attract guests that otherwise would not do interviews or be on a talk show. Even though Carson and Cavett had many of the same guests, Cavett was far more receptive to rock 'n' roll musicians than Carson. Having rock 'n' roll guests was unusual at the time. Jimi appeared on the show on September 9, 1969, only a few weeks after Woodstock. At that time, *The Dick Cavett Show* had been on the air for only a little over a year, since March 1968, as a daytime prime-time talk show. It didn't become a late-night talk show competitor to Carson's show until December 1969, four months after Jimi's appearance.

Jimi had also appeared on Cavett's show on July 7, 1969, about six weeks before Woodstock. I didn't see it. I don't think anybody did. The office never even mentioned it, and no one really knew it was airing. Jimi's September 9 appearance is the widely remembered one and often is referred to, incorrectly, as his only appearance.

Jimi originally had been booked to appear on Cavett's "Woodstock Show" on August 19, the day after the Woodstock concert. Jefferson Airplane, Joni Mitchell, and David Crosby and Stephen Stills of Crosby, Stills, Nash & Young all appeared on the show. Many of them came directly from the concert to the ABC studios in New York City, taping their appearances on the same afternoon that the show aired. Stephen Stills even pointed out that he still had mud on his pants from Woodstock. And a big controversy occurred during Jefferson Airplane's performance of "We Can Be Together": It marked the very first time the word "fuck" was uttered on national television. But the band members didn't stop there; they also sang the lyric "up against the wall, motherfucker."

David Crosby joined Jefferson Airplane on "Somebody to Love," and at the end of the show, the musicians, with the exception of Joni Mitchell, had an instrumental jam, and the audience got up and danced! Joni Mitchell never appeared at Woodstock. Her manager did not allow her to, because he was concerned that given the turmoil going at Woodstock, and the jammed New York State Thruway going to and from it, attending the festival could have prevented her from appearing on *The Dick Cavett Show*. He felt the show was way too important for her career and didn't want to risk her missing the taping of it. The irony is that Mitchell wrote the song "Woodstock," which is so closely identified with the concert event. She wrote it based on information and descriptions given to her by Graham Nash, and from the news images and reports she saw on television that dominated the airways that entire weekend. Crosby, Stills, Nash & Young recorded the song, and it was most famously used in the closing credits for the film *Woodstock*.

Jimi had been scheduled to appear with the others, but because the concert ran late, until Monday morning, he couldn't make it down to the taping. So the producers booked him to appear by himself a couple of weeks later.

I saw Jimi on the show. He was dressed rather flamboyantly—no surprise there. He was very soft-spoken and polite. He displayed a sense of humor and modestly downplayed his abilities. He was charming. In other words, he was being Jimi. He didn't fit the wild-man image that was his public persona. Cavett, of course, brought up Jimi's rendition of "The Star-Spangled Banner," referring to it as being unorthodox. Jimi defended the way he'd played it, saying it was "not unorthodox but beautiful." The audience applauded. Cavett blushed. To make up for it and make Jimi look patriotic, Cavett told the audience that Jimi had been in the Army, serving in the 101st Airborne Division as a paratrooper. Jimi politely acknowledged it but didn't elaborate.

The last thing I remember was Cavett trying to engage Jimi in a discussion about money after Jimi explained that he was a blues-based musician and that he loved the blues. Cavett asked Jimi if being a wealthy musician was contrary to the spirit of the blues. Jimi responded by saying, "It's easy to sing the blues when you have money." Oddly, Cavett never brought up the Harlem benefit concert that had taken place four days prior.

Late the next afternoon, I met with Jimi in the basement apartment at the East Thirty-Seventh Street office. We were supposed to decide whether or not we were going to continue with the script. When I got there, all Jimi did was complain about how Dick Cavett's people had pulled the plugs on a couple of his amps so the music wouldn't be too loud for the audience. I didn't want him to be upset by that, so I changed the subject, telling him I hadn't known he'd been an Airborne Ranger. Jimi wanted to talk about the Army. This was something he'd never done before. Maybe the Cavett show appearance had triggered something in him, so I figured, *What the hell?*

"Why did you join the Army?" I asked him.

I didn't expect the answer I got. "It was prison or the Army." He seemed amused by it.

He told me that when he was eighteen years old, the police had arrested him twice for riding in stolen cars. They didn't accuse him of stealing them, but that didn't matter. The judge gave him a choice between prison or joining the Army. He chose the Army and enlisted in May 1961. He was assigned to the 101st Airborne Division and stationed at Fort Campbell, Kentucky, as an Airborne Paratrooper. He talked about making parachute jumps, saying, "They were cool." He said he thought he'd made twenty-six parachute jumps and broken his ankle on the last one; because of that, he got a medical discharge in June 1962. Anyway, that was the "official" story he gave me.

However, Jimi was grateful that the Army had given him Billy Cox, and because of that it had all been worth it. Jimi had his guitar with him, and he would play at the Army club on base. Billy Cox, who was also a soldier at the same time, walked by one day and heard Jimi playing. He thought he was hearing John Lee Hooker, so he went in and introduced himself to Jimi as a fellow musician. Billy managed to get ahold of a bass guitar, and he and Jimi would jam together at every opportunity. That led them to perform at base clubs on weekends with other musicians. Jimi laughed when he said that they'd even had a band called the Casuals, because the group had just been thrown together.

Somehow this talk led to Vietnam. The war was raging at the time, and it was on everybody's mind, so I asked him how he felt about Vietnam, figuring I already knew the answer. His response was probably one of the most surprising things he ever said to me:

"I'm not really against the war."

Jimi was at first hawkish on the Vietnam War and felt it was necessary, but as we talked, his opinion changed. "I'm starting to wonder if this is a war to be dyin' in," he said.

As we discussed it further, Jimi revealed that what he cared about more than anything was the soldiers who were over there, fighting and suffering.

After a while he had to go, and I left, too. We didn't set a time to see each other again or to work on the script. I was now pretty sure that it wasn't going to happen. And again I questioned what I was doing there.

A couple of days later, I was in the neighborhood one evening, and, knowing that Kathy and Bob worked late, I decided to stop in and see if they had any idea what was going on with *Avril*. When I got there, Kathy was alone. I decided to complain to her about my working relationship with Jimi. One of my big complaints was that there was always a crowd of hangers-on around Jimi and nothing ever got done on *Avril*. I was starting to think the project was a waste of time.

She laughed and told me that I was being not only unrealistic but naive as well. She thought I was an idiot. She reminded me that Jimi Hendrix was one of the biggest rock stars in the world and that the groupies and hangers-on were part of the lifestyle. Not to mention that he was playing massive concerts like Woodstock, giving magazine interviews, doing TV shows, writing music, reforming his band, partying with friends and groupies, having a dozen girlfriends, looking for an apartment to rent in New York, and God knows what else.

"What did you expect?" she asked me. "What were you thinking?"

She accused me of refusing to accept the fact that Jimi had more important things to concern himself with than some side project that he'd come into on a whim. The fact that I was still in his life on some level surprised her. She'd thought it would last a week or two and Jimi would tire of it—get bored or distracted and move on to something else.

"The fact that you're still here means somehow you made a connection with Jimi, so just pick up your camera, do your moving in and out of here like a phantom so nobody really sees you but us, and be happy taking pictures," she said. "There aren't many people Jimi allows to take pictures of him recording in the studio. Wake up to reality, okay? Forget the script. Concentrate on being a photographer, because Jimi just doesn't have the time, so it's not going to happen."

"Well, I don't want to just hang around," was my lame response.

"Hang around? Are you kidding? Gimme a break. I think you came out of the same spy school Jeffery did. You're hardly ever here. You're so mysterious. Nobody knows who you are."

I just sat there with a dazed look on my face.

"I don't know what to say," I said finally.

"Well, I do. How long have you been coming around here?"
I shrugged.

"Would you like to see the other offices in the building?"
Her whole demeanor instantly changed.

"I don't know. I guess. Maybe."

"Trust me." She paused. "You do."

Kathy got up and walked toward the hall, not looking back, assuming that I would follow her. I did.

She led me into a corner office and shut the door.

"You want to smoke some weed?" she asked.

I didn't answer. She took a bag out of her purse, rolled a joint, lit it, took a hit, and handed it to me.

"Hawaiian," she said.

The more we smoked, the more we talked, giggled, then laughed. I was becoming paranoid about Bob. Soon I didn't care. Kathy was everything: witty, intelligent, funny, really attractive, and sexy. We talked and laughed about everything and anything. To me, Kathy was totally "it." A joint and a half later, maybe two, I was so stoned that I was no longer responsible for what I was saying or doing. I just didn't care. I think she was equally stoned. She stopped talking, walked up to me, pushed me down on the desk, and started tearing my clothes off. I feebly mumbled that Bob might come in.

"He won't," she said.

"How can you be so sure?"

"Because we're in Mike Jeffery's office."

I pulled her off the desk and pushed her down on the rug, each of us frantically pulling at each other's clothes. By the time we were on the rug, there wasn't much left to take off, and we got into a nonstop sex fest. Finally, exhausted and completely stoned, we collapsed.

I looked at her and asked, "Mike Jeffery's office?"

"Yup."

With that we both cracked up laughing, getting an extra charge from the fact that we'd just had uncontrollable, drug-induced sex in Mike Jeffery's office, and he would never know. There was something oddly perverted about that.

13

Salvatioη Club

One day in the fall of 1969, I took a subway to the West Village and got off at the Christopher Street stop. The main subway exit was in the middle of the street, so when I walked up the stairs and came out, I was in Sheridan Square, a bustling part of the West Village sandwiched between Bleeker Street and Seventh Avenue.

I did a 360-degree turn to take in everything going on around me, which was mostly people coming from somewhere or on their way to somewhere. Then halfway down the block, I saw a traffic cop writing a ticket next to a white Corvette Stingray, illegally parked in Sheridan Square. I thought it was Jimi's car, because he was the only person I knew who owned a car like that.

I chuckled to myself, "Not another ticket." I went over to the cop, because I had to let him know.

"Hey, the guy who owns that car is probably inside the building. It's Jimi Hendrix. You know, the…"

The cop didn't give a shit.

"Too late," he said. "Maybe the judge will like rock 'n' roll." He placed the ticket under the windshield wiper.

I remembered that Jimi had once mentioned a club in Sheridan Square called Salvation. He liked going there because nobody bothered him. It was small and below street level. I'd passed it hundreds of times but never gone in. It was located at One Sheridan Square and had a long, colorful history. The building itself was built in 1834, and over the years it had been a dining club (probably considered more upscale than a restaurant), a theater, a nightclub, and a disco.

Its claim to fame is that in 1938 it was a supper club called Café Society. I found it interesting that the owner hired John Hammond—a prominent jazz record producer and civil rights activist who became a talent scout—to find an unknown artist (because that's all the club could afford) to debut on the club's opening night. He brought in an unknown seventeen-year-old singer named Billie Holiday. Later in her career, Holiday remarked, "I opened at Café Society as an unknown; I left two years later a star."

She debuted her most famous song, "Strange Fruit," at Café Society; Jimi listed it as one of the most powerful pieces of music he'd ever heard. After finding Billie Holiday, Hammond went on to discover some of the greatest talents in music history, including Bob Dylan, Aretha Franklin, Leonard Cohen, Count Basie, Bruce Springsteen, and Stevie Ray Vaughan. Hammond was seventy-three years old when he signed Vaughan to a recording contract! He had a way of discovering new talent that no one else saw any potential in, and he had an unmatched instinct for raw musical talent. He single-handedly altered the course of American cultural history to become one of the most influential figures in twentieth-century popular music. He was inducted into the Rock & Roll Hall of Fame in 1986.

I think Jimi liked Salvation not only because he admired Billie Holiday, but because he felt a connection to the club's history. When it first opened its doors as Café Society, it was revolutionary. The owner refused to comply with the national racial segregation laws and welcomed mixed-race audiences and performers, which Jimi could relate to. Café Society became a cultural phenomenon. Jazz greats like Lena Horne, Sarah Vaughan, Art Tatum, "Big Joe" Turner, Count Basie, Nat King Cole, Les Paul, John Coltrane, Miles Davis, and even the legendary French singer Edith Piaf performed there.

Eventually, Café Society closed its doors. In the 1960s the place reopened as Salvation, a club co-owned by Jerry Schatzberg, a fashion photographer turned movie director. His club manager was Gennaro Sirrico, who later changed his name to Tony Sirico (yes, one "r") and played Pauli "Walnuts" Gualtieri on *The Sopranos*. Gennaro Sirrico was considered a low-level, gun-carrying shakedown artist who threatened to kill cops and claimed to have carried out a hit by putting five bullets in the victim's head. When he died in July 2022, his rap sheet listed twenty-eight arrests and two prison terms (and he'd had twenty-seven acting jobs as well).

Later, Salvation was driven into bankruptcy by the Mafia in what the police called a classic case of how members of organized crime move in on bars and nightspots, put their people on the payroll, and eventually take over. But before that happened, it flourished as a downstairs basement disco/nightclub where Andy Warhol and Lou Reed would hang out. Even John Lennon and Paul McCartney, along with entrepreneur Brian

Epstein's New York partner, Nat Weiss, had been there—and, of course, Jimi Hendrix.

I walked into Salvation that night in 1969 not knowing any of its past history or mob connections, but I knew Jimi was there, and I wanted to let him know that I'd tried to save him from getting a parking ticket. Much to my surprise, the club was nearly empty—maybe a dozen people. That would never have happened if cell phones had been everywhere, as they are today. People would have called and texted all their friends in the city, telling them to get down to the Village because Hendrix was there jamming. It would have turned into a mob scene. Instead, those who were lucky to be in whatever club Jimi selected to jam at were thrilled to witness and experience an intimate concert by a major rock star, who also was the world's greatest guitarist.

What people today probably can't relate to is that a major superstar would just show up unannounced at various clubs and assorted dives just to play spontaneously, then either hang out or leave. Jimi loved music more than anything in his life, and he didn't care if he was playing to thousands of people at Madison Square Garden or The Hollywood Bowl, or to hardly anyone at some cramped, smoked-filled dive in Greenwich Village. He just wanted to play. Money didn't matter to him; it was all about the music. This was one of the major problems Michael Jeffery had with Jimi, as I mentioned. For Jeffery, it was all about the money. It would infuriate him to learn that Jimi had shown up at some dive and played to a nonpaying crowd of maybe thirty people. Then the following week Jimi would play to a crowd of thousands of paying fans at Madison Square Garden or wherever.

Jimi was just finishing up playing an impromptu set on-stage at Salvation when I was sitting down at a rear table. I waved him over.

He sat down and remarked, "I didn't know you hung out here."

"I don't. I knew you were here. Just saw a cop putting a ticket on your car."

Jimi was unfazed, almost expecting it. "Just one?"

I then baited him, hoping to get a direct answer, something I rarely got from him. "Interesting visitors you had at the house," I said to him, referring to the guys with guys who'd stopped by Shokan House.

This was not the first time I heard him say this, nor would it be the last time. The words would be a little different, but the theme was always the same. It obviously weighed on Jimi's mind.

"Yeah. Had to be Jeffery set that shit up. Sent in some goons. They sit me down and tell me I've got to tour with The Experience. Can't break it up, can't form a new band, can't have a skin tone that's colored, that I might suffer 'irreparable bodily harm' if I try to change my music, whatever the hell that means."

"So what are you going to do?" I asked.

"I'm going to change my music."

Right about then, Jimi's on-and-off girlfriend Devon Wilson walked into the club. Her skin was almost gray, and she was so wasted that she couldn't walk in a straight line. Jimi was torn to see her but gave her his signature hug. I noticed that Devon's left hand smoothly slid something into Jimi's front pants pocket.

"Hey, baby," she slurred before yelling to the waitress in the corner, "I need a drink!"

She was unsteady as she sat down.

"You remember Jonathan?" Jimi asked her.

"No," she slurred, "'cause it's too damn hard to tell white faces apart." Then she turned to Jimi and said as if I weren't even there, let alone sitting next to her, "Jimi, what the hell do you need this cracker ass around for, anyway? You know he's nothing but a zit on your ass. You don't think this fuckface really cares about you? You realize, if you weren't a fuckin' rock star, he wouldn't even be..." and with that she passed out, her head going down on the table with a loud clunk. Jimi and I looked at each other, then we both started laughing. I moved the unconscious Devon a little farther away from me and him.

"Jimi, why do you keep her around?" I asked.

He paused. "Because she can score anything, anytime, anywhere."

"You mean like whatever it is she put in your pocket?"

"You picked up on that, huh?"

"Yeah, it wasn't hard to notice; she wasn't too subtle about it. You really want to have something on your person? What if you get pulled over for running a red light? A white Corvette Stingray in New York City is not exactly a car police can miss."

All of a sudden, I had visions of our film project's vanishing in another drug bust, so I said, "You've got to get rid of it. You want another Toronto in your life?"

"That fuckin' Devon. She's trying to get me hooked. She probably gets a bonus from her dealer if she gets me on it."

He then took three small glassine bags out of his left pocket. Two had pills; one had white powder. Jimi stared at the white powder.

129

"Are you kidding me?" I asked. "Are you doing H?"

"No man, no way."

"That can't be something you want," I said.

"It isn't. Not ever."

"Jimi, it will kill you, man."

Without saying a word, Jimi got up and went to the men's room. When he came back, he showed me a small empty cellophane bag.

"I flushed it," he said. "I don't need another Toronto. The only drug I need is my music. Music is my drug of choice."

I motioned to the waitress to bring us a couple more drinks. After two drinks, I decided to bring up a problem that had been eating away at me. I needed to get it out in the open, and now seemed like as good a time as any.

"I've got to talk to you about something," I said. "Uh, I've been doing Kathy—Kathy from the office."

Jimi's face took on a weird momentary look of surprise, then went blank. He asked, "How long have you been doing her?"

"About three months."

Then Jimi started laughing.

"What's so funny?" I asked. I hadn't expected this reaction.

"I was fuckin' her, too," Jimi said. That caught me completely off guard, and I didn't know what to say.

He went on, "but that's not what's so funny. Let me ask you something. Every time, she picks the place, right?"

"That's right."

"Every single time, right?"

"Yeah, always."

"I guarantee you Bob has been watching every time you did it with her."

Jimi (left), Billy Cox (middle), and guitarist Larry Lee (right). Lee was an old pal of Jimi's and joined Gypsy Sun and Rainbows primarily as a rhythm player.

Jimi's hands were always a blur.

Jimi rehearsing for Woodstock at the Hit Factory.

At the Hit Factory, summer 1969. Jimi didn't mind me getting close.

Jimi lost in his playing.

Jimi was captivating from any angle.

Jimi jamming with Gypsy Sun and Rainbows at the Hit Factory, rehearsing for Woodstock.

Bassist Billy Cox watching Jimi play a solo during rehearsals.

That's the back of my head far right. I'm talking to Jimi during a break at rehearsals at the Hit Factory in the summer of 1969 before Woodstock.

That's Jimi's pal Billy Cox rehearsing about a month before Woodstock. With the new group, Gypsy Sun and Rainbows, Jimi was teaching them all the new songs.

I loved being able to shoot Jimi at Woodstock.

Jimmy deep in thought just before he begins to play his iconic version of "The Star-Spangled Banner."

This is the moment Jimi took the stage at Woodstock. It took him a couple of seconds to process what was happening out there in front of him.

Slightly blown out shot, but gives a sense of how crowded the stage was at Woodstock.

Many people had left Woodstock by the time Jimi arrived to play.

This was a favorite shot of Jimi's that I took at Woodstock. The New York Times Magazine *often ran photos that were out of focus as a creative statement. He called this his* "New York Times Magazine *shot." He smiled when he caught me in his view.*

"*What?* No way. You can't know that."

Jimi was now enjoying my reaction to this revelation. "I can. 'Cause once when I was fucking her in the office, the guy went to sleep and fell out of the closet."

As if the first piece of information weren't mind-blowing enough, this caused me to crash and burn. Jimi knew it by the stunned look on my face.

"So what are you going to do, stop seeing her?" he asked.

It took an eternity for me to get the words out. "No, I can't. I'm completely taken with her. She's fantastic. I've never met anyone like her. And what you just said doesn't matter. I can't stop. What about you?"

"No, it was a brief fling. It's over. But I know what you mean, man. She's one great chick. Not many around like her, but what's that they say? 'Don't shit where you drink' or something like that. Man, come on, she works in my office. I see her every time I'm there. It's a recipe for disaster. There's no future in it. Besides, Devon would cut my balls off."

Then he added, "You know Kathy will never leave Bob Levine. She loves him more than anything in this world. You haven't got a chance."

That jolted me back to reality. I completely forgot about Devon, even though she was practically asleep in my lap by now.

"Come on, let's get out of here," Jimi said.

Motioning to the passed-out Devon, I said, "What about her?"

Jimi handed a passing waiter several twenty-dollar bills. "Hey, man, can I ask you to take out some trash for me?" We left her there passed out on the table.

131

Out in front of the club, Jimi stopped to light a cigarette and said, "Man, if you don't use, how come you know so much about drugs?"

"That's a conversation for a whole other day."

Just then, a dirty, ragged hippie with a stained shirt that read "Love" emerged from the shadows to confront Jimi. "Hey, you, Jimi Hendrix! I paid eighteen goddamn bucks to see you at Woodstock. That shouldn't have cost me anything, not a penny."

Jimi didn't flinch. "Look, man, a lot of beautiful things happened there."

"Fuck you," said the hippie, who was obviously high. "Music should be free to everybody! All of it! Everyone, the whole earth, man." He reminded me of the jerk after the concert backstage at Woodstock, only more wasted. Ignoring him, Jimi nodded goodbye to me, took his parking ticket, hopped in his Corvette, and drove away.

The hippie yelled after him, *"Where's my fuckin' Corvette?"*

I turned around and started walking back to my apartment, thinking that this whole thing had just happened with Jimi because I'd seen a cop writing up a parking violation. It had to be fate. As I was walking away, I heard a commotion behind me being caused by the stoner. I turned around. He was blocking the path of a tall, striking brunette with an astoundingly toned body, carrying a small pink suitcase. I watched as she kept trying to go around him, but he kept blocking her path. She became more and more frustrated and upset. I had to do something.

"Excuse me, is this asshole bothering you?" I asked. Just by the look on her face, I knew the answer. "Yeah, I thought so."

I grabbed his wrist and whipped his arm up high behind his back, and then I ran him to a nearby trash can and dumped him in it headfirst, his legs kicking in the air. He was so stoned, I don't think he even knew what had happened. It might have looked dramatic, but because of his condition, it was pretty easy to do; it was like moving a lump of Jell-O. But it made me look like a hero. At least that's what I was hoping for.

"Hey, you okay?" I asked the woman. "Can I buy you a drink or...?"

"Sorry, I've had a really long day." She handed me a card. "Come by the club and I'll buy you one. I'm Jenny." Then she turned and walked away.

As she was walking away, I looked down at the card. It had her name, Jenny, and "Playboy Club—New York City."

14

Kidnapped

A couple of days later, I called the office and learned that Jimi had been kidnapped! I thought it was a joke, and Kathy tried to treat it as if it were only a rumor. Two days later, Jimi was back in the office looking fine, and the office was back to normal, so I asked him, "Kidnapped?"

Jimi's response was, "Don't ask."

It would be months before I learned anything more about it. Jimi, Kathy, Bob Levine, and Mike Jeffery wouldn't discuss it. I found out through the grapevine that one night when Jimi was at Salvation, he was grabbed outside the club by two wannabe wise guys. They took him to a house somewhere, called the office, and demanded something. I never did find out what the something was.

Supposedly, John Riccobono, the Mafia man who operated the Salvation (and I'd once heard Michael Jeffery mention the name), and his mob partner found out the names of Jimi's kidnappers and threatened that if they didn't release Jimi, they would be dead by morning. Jimi was released after about two days.

Riccobono later changed his name to Jon Roberts to hide from law enforcement. It's been said that he was a serious mobster. His father was a member of La Cosa Nostra (the Sicilian Mafia), and Riccobono/Roberts ended up spearheading the Medellín drug cartel's rise in the 1980s and becoming a convicted cocaine trafficker. Jimi never confirmed or denied being kidnapped, so I really don't know if it happened. It was never mentioned again, except one time by Kathy, who said that she believed that the kidnapping might have been set up by Jeffery to send a message to Jimi not to try to seek new representation.

One afternoon, the phone in my apartment rang. When I answered it and verified who I was, the man on the other end identified himself as FBI. He let me know the call was being recorded and other people were listening. They hit me with one question after another—not rapidly, but in a slow, methodical monotone, almost as if I were on the witness stand in a courtroom. They wanted to know about my relationship with Jimi Hendrix. At the time, Richard Nixon was president, and government agents were investigating almost anyone they perceived as a radical.

"Were you party to any discussions concerning the Black Panthers?" the agent asked.

"No."

"Is Mr. Hendrix involved in any so-called underground movements or radical organizations?"

"I don't know. All I was doing was writing a movie script, and now I'm taking pictures. I'm not involved in anything he does."

"Do you believe that Mr. Hendrix's rendition of 'The Star-Spangled Banner' is an unpatriotic act?"

The question made me laugh. I found it totally absurd.

"Can you describe the relationship between Mr. Hendrix and Mr. Michael Jeffery?"

"His relationship? He's Jimi's manager. Everybody knows that, and probably you do, too. So why are you asking me?"

I don't remember any of the other questions or how long the call went on, but I remember that as we were hanging up, they warned me that they would be watching me.

I told them, "Go ahead, knock yourself out. I guarantee you'll be bored."

When I hung up, I realized what had just happened and freaked out. The first thing I did was grab a joint.

Sometime afterward I went into the office, and much to my surprise, Jimi was there. I asked to speak to him in private, and we went downstairs.

"I got a call about you from the FBI," I told him.

"Yeah, I know," he said—a response I didn't expect.

"You know?"

"The office told me that I'm being investigated. They called here a couple times. They're looking at me because of the Panthers, and about how they think my music is getting to white people. They think I'm something like a spy from the Panthers trying to brainwash all the white kids."

In my head, this was turning into a bad script.

"Like, because it's easy for me to cross some kind of deep race divide," Jimi continued. "I've been feeling that I'm being watched by somebody. Not in London, only in New York." He speculated that maybe Jeffery was using his intelligence connections to set him up. But this paranoia was probably the result of the enormous amount of stress he was under because of the looming court case for his Toronto drug bust. Even though no one spoke about it, it hung heavily over the office.

So the FBI began investigating Jimi in 1969, a little before the call I got. This was during the height of the Vietnam War and the civil rights movement. Jimi wasn't really a vocal critic of the war, but the FBI took his performance of "The Star-Spangled Banner" at Woodstock as an indication that he was. However, Jimi supported the civil rights movement. Additionally, the FBI was under the impression that Jimi was associating with members of the Black Panther Party, a political organization that the FBI also was investigating.

The FBI's interest in Hendrix was confirmed in 1970, when the agency opened a file on him. The file, which was released to the public in 2010 under the Freedom of Information Act, contains over two hundred pages of documents related to Jimi and his activities. The documents reveal that the FBI's interest in Jimi was related primarily to his political views and associations. But the FBI's investigation of Jimi was not limited to monitoring his political activities. They also collected information about his personal life, including his drug use and his relationships with women, likely motivated by a desire to discredit him and undermine his supposed influence on young people.

Despite the FBI's efforts to discredit Jimi, they failed. Jimi remained a beloved and influential figure in popular culture. His music continues to inspire new generations of musicians, and his legacy as a pioneer of rock 'n' roll is secure. The FBI's investigation of Jimi is now seen as a relic of a bygone era, part of the great lengths the government went to in an effort to silence dissenting voices.

It's a fascinating but disturbing chapter in the history of rock 'n' roll, when the most celebrated and influential figures in popular culture became targets of government surveillance and harassment. The most famous and most visible target was John Lennon. Almost no one was aware that Jimi was also the target of an investigation. Regardless, it didn't bother him or affect him. He just ignored it and continued what he was doing—just being Jimi.

15

Toronto Drug Bust

It wasn't until after the Toronto drug-bust case was over that I learned all the details. Here's what happened. The Jimi Hendrix Experience had been scheduled to perform in Toronto, and someone tipped them off that there was the possibility of a drug bust. Jimi's tour managers, Gerry and Tony, warned Jimi. He told them he didn't have any drugs on him or in his bag. Regardless, just prior to landing in Toronto, the concert promoter, Terry, told Jimi to get rid of whatever he had in his bag. Supposedly, Terry then took Jimi into the plane's bathroom and dumped anything that might be mistaken for illegal drugs into the toilet, even though what they flushed down the toilet wasn't drugs. Terry didn't care; he wanted to play it safe.

After the plane landed at the Toronto international airport on May 3, 1969, Jimi and Terry were the last to exit. Tony was carrying Jimi's bags, and he placed them on a counter at the customs station. The customs agent shouted at him not to touch it if it wasn't his bag. Tony told the customs agent that he worked for Jimi, but the agent repeated his order. Tony backed away, and the agent asked Jimi if they were his bags. Jimi said they were. After the customs officials went through his bag, Jimi was detained because they had found a small amount of what they suspected to be drugs in it.

They set up a mobile lab to determine what the substance was. It turned out to be heroin and hashish. The police placed Jimi under arrest for illegal possession of narcotics, and he was booked, fingerprinted, and photographed. During this whole time, Gerry was frantically trying to locate Mike Jeffery, but Jeffery was on his way to Hawaii and couldn't be reached. Gerry then contacted the management at the venue for the concert that was scheduled for that night, the Toronto Maple Leaf Gardens. Upon hearing what had happened, the managers pressured the Toronto police department to release Jimi, complaining that the sell-out crowd of eighteen thousand fans might riot if they canceled the show. Jimi was released on $10,000 bail and required to return on May 5 for an arraignment hearing, and then again for a preliminary hearing in June.

Jimi was released by eight p.m. and escorted straight to the Toronto Maple Leaf Gardens by the police, who remained at the arena throughout the performance. That night, The Jimi Hendrix Experience gave a great performance, and Jimi was in great spirits, even joking with the audience, which he rarely ever did. He altered the lyrics to "Red House," singing, "Soon as I get out of jail, I wanna see her."

When Jimi showed up for the arraignment hearing on May 5, which lasted for all of three minutes, the courthouse was filled with young fans who had come to show their support for him. Jimi entered wearing a pink shirt open to the waist, an

Apache-style headband, a multicolored scarf, and beads. Mike Jeffery was livid about the outfit, believing it called unnecessary attention to Jimi. At the preliminary hearing, a date was set for Jimi to stand trial for two counts of illegal possession of narcotics.

The anxiety it caused around the office was understandable, and it created a weird vibe. Jimi, if convicted, could face up to twenty years in prison.

On June 19, 1969, Jimi flew to Toronto for a preliminary hearing. This time he wore a business suit. It was the first time he'd worn a suit since 1966. The date December 8 was set for Jimi to stand trial for two counts of possession of heroin and hashish. More serious potential charges of drug transporting and trafficking, which had been discussed at the time of the arrest, were not filed.

During this time, I occasionally stopped by the office, more to see Kathy than Jimi. I didn't even know he was in town, but he was there and he'd had a haircut; it was the shortest I had ever seen his hair. I remarked to Kathy about it, and she said that it was for the trial. This was the first time I'd heard anything about it.

"What trial?" I asked.

She didn't answer me. Instead, she found something else to do and ignored me, so I figured it was something very private. I left, but not before I saw Bob Levine leaving before me to take Jimi shopping.

In preparation for the trial, not only did Jimi have his hair cut, but he bought new clothes. Bob Levine took Jimi to a number of stores in New York that specialized in tailored suits. They found a conservative suit that looked great on Jimi. Jimi hated it. He was totally uncomfortable and was constantly trying to loosen his tie. Levine didn't care how uncomfortable he was; he thought the suit was perfect.

The day before the trial, Levine made a point to personally take Jimi to the airport for the trip to Toronto. On the way, he reminded Jimi that they would be going through customs and that he'd better not bring anything suspicious on board. According to Levine, Jimi reassured him that he wouldn't. Levine questioned what was in Jimi's guitar case, reminding him that they would be searched at customs. The way Levine told it later, Jimi insisted that he (Levine) had nothing to worry about, telling him that no one was going to recognize him.

Levine could not believe that Jimi believed this to be true and told him that not only would customs agents recognize him—haircut or no haircut, suit or no suit—but that they would be waiting at customs for him. Sure enough, soon after their arrival at the Toronto airport, Jimi was arrested by customs agents, who found a capsule of an unknown substance in his guitar case. They put Jimi in jail, where he spent the night waiting for it to be tested. The next day, the police dropped the charges when it was determined to be a legal medication.

You have to understand the times. In 1969, Toronto was very conservative, and it was being overrun by hippies from the States moving there to avoid the draft. Many Canadian officials were antagonistic about it. They looked with suspicion upon anybody who looked or dressed differently from themselves. Jimi fit both criteria.

Jimi's defense attorney during the trial made a point of bringing up the presence of the Royal Canadian Mounted Police at the airport. The Mounties did not typically make arrests at the airport. The defense attorney speculated that

Jimi had been purposedly targeted by the Canadian authorities, and that they intentionally had searched Jimi in plain
view of people at the airport to create a public spectacle.

There was no question as to whether the drugs had been
in Jimi's luggage, but in order for the prosecutors to prove
possession, they had to show that Jimi had known they were
there. The customs officer who discovered the drugs and the
lab technicians who identified them as heroin didn't know
whether he'd known it or not. Upon cross-examination, Jimi's
lawyer, John O'Driscoll, raised doubts about whether the
drugs had belonged to Jimi, and presented a case that Jimi
had been singled out by customs because of the flamboyant
way he'd been dressed.

The customs agent who discovered the drugs did, in fact,
agree with Jimi's attorney that Jimi had drawn attention to
himself at the airport by wearing "obviously mod clothing."
The customs agent stated that Jimi hadn't had any drug paraphernalia in his luggage, and he confirmed that when he
examined Jimi, he found no needle tracks on his arms.

Jimi's defense team did not dispute that the drugs had been
found in his bag. They instead developed a strategy to prove
that he had not been aware of the bag's contents. They did
that by providing numerous accounts of how common it was
for Jimi to receive gifts from fans, which often included drugs.
When Jimi was on the stand, he testified that fans showered
gifts on him, including teddy bears, scarves, clothing, and
jewelry, and he explained that while he'd been in Los Angeles,
a female fan had given him a vial, which he put in his bag—as
he always did with gifts from fans—without any knowledge of
its contents or even thinking about it. He just threw it in his
bag and forgot about it, then boarded the plane for Toronto.

This sent the prosecutor into attack mode, and he tried to tear Jimi's testimony apart on the grounds that Jimi could not have been so stupid and so naive as to not know what fans were giving him. He asked, did he really know how it had gotten into his bag, or even who had put it there? Jimi's simple response was "yes."

Both of Jimi's bandmates, Mitch Mitchell and Noel Redding, believed that the drugs had been planted in Jimi's bag. When asked about his drug use, Jimi denied that he had ever used heroin or amphetamines but admitted to smoking pot and hashish. Jimi also admitted that he had used cocaine twice and LSD a couple of times, but added that his days of smoking pot were almost over because "I feel I have outgrown it."

During the trial, Jimi's defense attorney raised doubts about whether the narcotics actually belonged to Jimi because it had been verified that Jimi had had no drug paraphernalia in his luggage and no needle tracks on his arms, which proved he was not an addict and did not shoot up heroin. It came out that Jimi had an extreme fear of needles, which discouraged him from using heroin, plus his association with junkies in the music industry over the years had convinced him it was not a drug he wanted to ever use. If anything, Jimi was anti-heroin.

The trial lasted for three days. The jury deliberated for eight hours before returning a "not guilty" verdict, acquitting Jimi of both charges. Jimi came back from Toronto elated. He'd beat the rap.

Jimi later referenced his arrest in lyrics he wrote for "Stepping Stone": "Flying can't be trusted—got busted." Many other rock stars were busted in Toronto as well. Toronto customs agents were known to go hard on rock stars.

In 2018, the fingerprint card from Jimi's booking at the police station was placed up for auction. It was sold on March 15, 2018, for $29,248.10.

16

The Generation Club and Electric Lady Studios

Jimi Hendrix would have turned eighty in November 2022. In his twenty-seven years on this earth and with his even briefer musical career, Jimi left an indelible mark on guitar playing and rock music. He single-handedly and permanently transformed both art forms, but he believed that his most lasting impact on music would come from a project completed just three weeks before his death: the founding of Electric Lady Studios, a state-of-the-art recording studio located at 52 West Eighth Street in New York's Greenwich Village. It became the first and only artist-owned recording studio in the world. The idea is common today, but in 1969 it was radical. It's fitting that Jimi did it first. And had personally supervised many of the details.

Originally Jimi wanted to buy a nightclub called the Generation Club. It was a popular Greenwich Village spot where he would drop in unannounced and jam with whoever was playing. On the night of April 7, 1968, Jimi jammed with Roy Buchanan. There were other bands and musicians there that night—including Big Brother and the Holding Company with Janis Joplin, and Buddy Guy—but Jimi didn't jam with them. *Monterey Pop* documentary filmmaker D. A. Pennebaker— whom, coincidentally, I had been introduced to in an elevator at the Film Center a week before—was there, and he filmed the jam sessions. He had invited me to come down to the club that night; if I'd gone, I would have met Jimi for the first time.

Pennebaker made an unreleased short documentary film called *Wake at Generation*. It was a concert film that featured Janis and Big Brother and the Holding Company performing their classic rendition of "Summertime," legendary folk singer Joni Mitchell performing "Sisotowbell Lane," bluesman Buddy Guy doing "Stormy Monday," Jimi with Hugh McCracken and B. B. King along with Paul Butterfield and Elvin Bishop, and then Richie Havens doing "All Along the Watchtower/Sing This All Together." In the film, Jimi can be seen recording the other performances on a reel-to-reel recorder.

I knew very little about the Generation Club initially during the time Jimi and I were hanging out. I learned about it only because one time during one of our back-and-forth creative sessions for the script, Jimi asked me what I thought of it. I only knew that a well-publicized wake for the Reverend Martin Luther King Jr. had been held there.

"We bought it," Jimi told me.

"'We'?" I asked.

"Yeah, me and Mike Jeffery."

Talk about being blindsided.

"*Mike Jeffery?*" The very manager whose grip Jimi wanted to break.

147

"I know what you're thinking, but we bought it a year ago." He paused, deep in thought, then said softly while looking down at the floor, "Sometimes you have to make a pact with the devil to get what you want."

Well, I guess so, and he did.

Jimi explained his vision for Electric Lady. "A living room. It's going to feel like a living room. No sharp angles, and art on the walls everywhere. Not just a studio but also a club, so I can perform and record at the same time."

I would later learn that in late 1968, Mike Jeffery and Jimi had decided to open a combination nightclub and recording studio club together in the Village. Jeffery had put $50,000 down on the Generation Club, a favorite hangout of Jimi's.

In one of the few surprisingly civil conversations I had with Mike Jeffery, he told me he was all for it. He saw it as a way to make more money, and he could make sure all the cash flowed to him. He agreed to bankroll the venture. What Jimi didn't know at the time, but would learn later on, was that none of it was Jeffery's money, even though Jeffery wanted him to think it was. Jeffery had gone to Jimi's label, Reprise, owned by Warner's, and somehow had gotten Warner's on board to fund the venture. I can only imagine what he said to them, or what misrepresentations he made to have them agree to it.

Even though I was aware of the club, I had never been there. But everybody knew the Generation Club, especially musicians. The more he frequented the club, the more Jimi dreamed about owning it and turning it into a hybrid nightclub, but to do this he needed money. Enter Mike Jeffery.

Jeffery was intrigued with the building and started researching it. He found out that it had been designed and built in 1929 as a movie theater called the Film Guild Cinema. It was designed by an avant-garde architect named Frederick Kiesler, who envisioned it as the "first 100 percent cinema," and he incorporated features of modernist design.

Jeffery loved the fact that the building had a long history before Jimi chanced upon it. In 1930, the basement of the building was called The Village Barn, a country-themed nightclub and dining hall that lasted from 1930 to 1967. Jeffery let anyone who was willing to listen know that the Village Barn had even spawned the first country music program on American network television (NBC) that didn't originate out of Nashville. Go figure. The TV show ran from 1948 to 1950 and featured weekly performances from the likes of Pappy Howard and His Tumbleweed Gang, Harry Ranch and His Kernels of Korn, and even the governor of Oklahoma, Roy J. Turner, who performed his single "My Memory Trail." It was so out of place in New York City that everyone loved it. If nothing else, you had to go just to say you'd been.

Being interested in art, Jeffery was fascinated by the fact that the Abstract Expressionist painter Hans Hofmann had lectured in an upstairs studio from 1938 through the 1950s, contemporaneously with the Village Barn's TV run. Keeping up with the cinematic theme of the building, it eventually became the Eighth Street Playhouse, an art house movie theater, until 1992. The Eight Street Playhouse invented midnight showings. It screened the *Rocky Horror Picture Show*, accompanied by the film's famous floor show, every Friday and Saturday night for eleven years. I saw my first John Sayles movie, *Return of the Secaucus 7*, at that theater. Years later, I ended up living in the same neighborhood as Sayles in Hoboken, New Jersey.

When Jimi and Mike Jeffery acquired the club, the entrance was unique in that it had a brick facade that stuck out onto the sidewalk like somebody's fat belly. Electric Lady Studios kept the façade. It was unmistakable, a holdover from the Generation Club days, and it made the club stand out.

Originally Jimi said that he wanted to keep the nightclub intact and use it as a place to jam and hang out. He envisioned a recording booth in the club where he could record live. That changed when Jimi, Jeffery, and Eddie Kramer (Jimi's recording engineer) came up with the idea of designing and renovating the space as a state-of-the-art recording studio. At that time label-controlled studios were the norm, and it cost a fortune every time Jimi recorded. Electric Lady had the promise of financial salvation and would be a recording industry first, an artist-controlled, full-service recording studio.

Design and construction took all of 1969 and went well into 1970. Jimi once told me that the total cost was over a million dollars (today that would be $7.8 million).

Eddie Kramer would later become Jimi's record producer, and he deserves some of the credit for Electric Lady Studios, because he helped convince Jimi to focus on building a recording studio. Kramer was very familiar with Jimi's quirky nature and need to find the perfect recording environment. He knew that Jimi was notorious for forgetting to properly manage his time while recording, sometimes doing as many as twenty takes to get one note "right." He and Jeffery also were aware of the staggering studio fee for recording the *Electric Ladyland* album.

Jimi insisted on redesigning the space as a unique recording studio, one that would be ideal for his creativity. Nobody, not even The Beatles, owned their recording studio.

The trio found an unknown, untried, and inexperienced twenty-three-year-old designer-architect named John Storyk, a recent Princeton University graduate, to be the designer-architect for Electric Lady Studios. Storyk had not designed anything except for school projects. For Electric Lady, he proposed designing walls with warm curves and psychedelic murals. Jimi related to his designs and concepts immediately, and the next thing anyone knew, Storyk was designing a major recording studio for a major rock star as his first job out of college.

Mike Jeffery knew that it was going to take a mountain of cash to finish the work, and he made plans to have Jimi tour like a fool to foot the bill. Jeffery wanted to make sure that it would be Jimi's money going toward the work, not his.

One day in February 1970, Jimi took me down to the building site. There was a big problem. The downstairs space had flooded during a rainstorm, which revealed that the building was over an arm of an old underground river. Pumps had to be installed permanently to keep the space dry, and now sound insulation had to be put around the pumps to kill the noise. I hadn't known that New York City even had underground rivers. At the same time, battles of will were going on between Jimi and Jeffery, and there were major disagreements with the record label as the pressure to meet contract deadlines began building. On top of it all, there never seemed to be enough money for the next phase of the studio project.

The day Jimi took me to the jobsite was when I met John Storyk for the first time. He seemed so young, but then again, we all were. The little time I spent around Storyk watching him work, I was convinced he was a genius. He knew exactly what Jimi wanted, and Eddie Kramer knew exactly what Jimi needed. The two of them were the perfect team for the studio project.

Storyk wanted to design and build the space as Jimi's dream home. He didn't want the studio to have any straight lines; all the walls were curved. It was Jimi's idea to make the studio look and feel like a living room. Jimi once told me that the unique facade of Electric Lady Studios was John Storyk's idea, and that he had been inspired by the building's original architect, Kiesler—especially by Kiesler's design for the famous museum in Israel that houses the Dead Sea Scrolls.

Jimi had a lot to do with the design of Electric Lady Studios. The space certainly was one of a kind. It's been described as a psychedelic lair of sorts, with multicolor lights, erotic sci-fi paintings and posters, and curved walls. And it would have analog rather than digital recording and editing equipment.

Once again, Jimi and I decided to make some time, if only a couple of hours, to work on the script. Well, the work never happened. Jimi was booked solid. Jimi was touring. Jimi was recording. Jimi had an interview. One thing after the other. No downtime. I knew it was Mike Jeffery's doing.

Frustrated, I went to Jimi's office, not knowing what I was going to accomplish other than venting to Bob Levine. He wasn't there. Kathy was. I started complaining to her.

"I'm frustrated," I told her. "I set a time with Jimi to do some work on the script, and he canceled without letting me know. This is not the way you write a script. This is not how it works!"

Unfazed, Kathy dryly remarked: "You're naive, aren't you? You just don't learn. Did you think that a major rock star like Jimi Hendrix would be reliable? And that writing a script is a priority? Please!"

"Well, yeah...I did."

"I'll say it again: You're naive. Didn't we go over this before? It's déjà vu. He's booked solid. He's touring. He will be recording. He's doing interviews. Somebody needs to pay for Electric Lady."

"Yeah, but I thought Mike Jeffery was handling all of that, that it's coming from the label. I don't understand."

"Nope, you sure don't. How do you think Mike is paying for building the studio? Do you know how much that's costing?"

"Not really."

"No, you sure don't. Do you think that Reprise is covering all the costs? With all the construction problems? No way. I know you're like the "accidental tourist" here, but wake up. You know that Jeffery never puts a dime of his own money into anything. And if you don't, I'm telling you now that Jimi pays for everything. He pays for this office. He pays for Mike, for Bob, and for me. And Jeffery makes sure of that. It all comes from touring, recordings, personal appearances."

The more she talked, the more I realized she was a strong, tough, take-charge, smart, realistic, no-nonsense woman. She had everything under control. She had her shit together, much more than I did. And it made her much more desirable, more beautiful in my eyes.

As she was talking, she approached me and stood directly in front of me. "Look, I know you didn't ask for any of this, that you were unexpectedly thrown into all of this, but don't give me your innocent 'I want to stay under the radar and am not a part of his entourage' bullshit again, because I'm tired of it. Well, guess what? You are. As long as you hang out with him, as long as you show up at recording sessions, go to his apartment or hotel or wherever, the Ashokan house, go to his parties, you are part of his entourage. So wake up, darling... and enjoy the ride."

She ran her fingers through my hair, then pushed me away, straightened up, and looked at me, not saying a word.

This was her fiancé's office. I knew it was the era of free love and women's lib, but I was filled with guilt.

"Listen, Kathy, we can't do this anymore.... I can't do this anymore."

She looked right through me and was cool. "Okay. Sure."

Then she casually turned around and went back to her office, saying: "Close the door on the way out."

I did. I was glad no one was around the office that day, and left the building. In the cab on the way back to my apartment, I became very depressed. I had "broken up" with Kathy, but she had never really been mine to begin with, and we had never really been in a real boyfriend-girlfriend relationship. She was engaged, for God's sake, and there was no way in hell she would leave Bob for me or anyone else, so why did I feel this way? I'd created a fantasy, and she never had. She was a realist. I was the foolish dreamer. It was time to move on.

17

Jenny

Around the same time that I "broke up" with Kathy, I had to give up my apartment on Bethune Street in the Village. It was a sublet, and the woman who had the lease wanted the place back. Fortunately, not right away; she gave me ninety days to find another place and move out. Through a friend, I got a tip on an 1,800-square-foot loft in Hoboken, New Jersey, right across the river from New York, for five hundred dollars a month. It was a phenomenal place, but I hated the idea of not being in the Village, until I learned that there was a PATH train station only ten blocks away. The train would get me to the Village in nine minutes. I rented the loft.

Depressed over the *Avril* script's hardly moving forward, the breakup with Kathy, and having to move out of New York—even though it would be another three months—I went on a self-destructive bender of marijuana, booze, and women nonstop for two weeks. I ended up admitting myself to St. Peter's University Hospital in Jersey City, New Jersey, with early signs of pneumonia. I picked St. Peter's because my uncle was a doctor there and could get me in. That turned out to be a mistake, because he continually nagged me for being so stupid and ending up in the hospital.

Once I was out of the hospital, I went back to the Bethune Street apartment, determined to enjoy the last three months there. While walking down Twelfth Street, a block from my apartment, I ran into Jenny, the girl I'd met outside Salvation who worked at the Playboy Club. I recognized her, and she recognized me. We got into a conversation, and I invited her to go down the street to the White Horse Tavern for a glass of wine. She was really attractive, a girl-next-door type, who was, in fact, very sweet and not at all worldly, and had a hint of innocence that was a refreshing change from the groupie types. She asked what I did for a living, and I told her I was a photographer and script writer. She asked me what I was writing and who I took pictures of, and I told her—almost under my breath, because I was not out to impress her with my tie to Jimi.

To my complete surprise, she didn't know who Jimi Hendrix was! She didn't follow contemporary music, didn't even listen to it. She was a classically trained pianist and spent her time listening to and enjoying classical music. She had no interest in rock or even jazz.

We exchanged numbers and said we hoped to get together again sometime.

Since I was on West Twelfth Street and Electric Lady was on West Eighth Street, I decided to stop in to see where the construction was at. Once there, I found out that it was still not going well. I decided that it didn't involve me, and no one there knew what I was even doing there, so I left.

I decided to get on with my life and step away from the whole script-writing project and Jimi Hendrix thing, and I stopped going to the office. Jenny and I began dating. She was wonderful to be with. The best thing about it was that I didn't have to share her with anyone. One day she approached me and asked me if I would drive her to her parents' house in New Jersey. Of course, I said yes. On the drive there, she warned me to not be surprised by the unexpected, and to be prepared to accept anything that might happen. I questioned her about it, and Jenny responded, "My parents aren't your normal parents. They're a bit strange."

She introduced me to her parents when we got there, and I couldn't understand what she had been talking about; her parents seemed normal and nice to me. They offered me a drink and explained that friends from the neighborhood would be dropping by for a pool party and I was welcome. Jenny was in the corner of the room straining her neck to get my attention and motioning me to say no. I ignored her. These were nice people. I thought it would be nice to be in a normal environment, an escape from the insanity of the world of rock 'n' roll. Jenny gave up and left the room.

Her parents continued talking to me. Some of their guests arrived, two suburban New Jersey couples. They all came into the living room. Her parents were especially fixated on me, and I assumed they were scoping me out for their daughter, to make sure I wasn't some sort of druggie or weirdo. Then without warning, and so matter-of-factly that it took me several minutes to process it, they all took off their clothes. Standing in front of me were six naked middle-aged people. They invited me to join them. I was shocked, embarrassed, and speechless all at once. Jenny popped her head into the room and mouthed "I warned you." They were nudists.

Later the backyard nudist pool party grew to nearly two dozen people, all naked, including me. I was sitting on a lounge chair chatting uncomfortably with Jenny's naked mother. Jenny was nowhere to be found, and I was too embarrassed to get up and go look for her. Then she appeared from inside the house and walked across the patio to the diving board, naked. Her body was amazing. She had an even, golden tan, not one bathing suit mark on her. As her mother and I watched Jenny jump off the diving board, her mother said, "Doesn't she have a beautiful body?"

Jenny and I drove back to NYC the next morning. I never went back to that house, and I never saw her parents again. If Jenny had asked me to drive her out to New Jersey to her parents' house again, my answer would have been a resounding no.

18

The Limo Incident

I passed some of my photographer responsibilities off to my friend Mike Viapiana, a real photographer and someone who Jimi knew and was comfortable with. During this time, I was trying to help Jimi with his management problem, and I reached out to a good friend, Steve Schwartz, whose brother-in-law was a top New York attorney. With Jimi's permission, I invited Steve to come down to meet Jimi at a recording session. Steve never came into the recording session. He stayed in the hallway so as not to be an intrusion. When Jimi took a slight break, I had to bring him out to the hallway to introduce him to Steve. Steve listened to Jimi and learned about the stranglehold Jeffery had on him—how it was affecting him and his creativity, not to mention the business dealings between them. Steve said, "My brother-in-law can help you."

Jimi gave Steve the office number to pass on to the attorney, then he went back to the recording session. I decided to stay and shoot some pictures of Jimi recording, telling Steve I would meet him in an hour at a bar on the corner. I eventually did, but we left that bar and went to a funky neighborhood bar, had a few drinks, and caught up on things.

I decided to go back to the office; it didn't feel right to stay away. I had really been avoiding it only because I was afraid to run into Kathy, which was unavoidable, but I had used the excuse that I wanted to get on with my life and move away from the script and the whole Jimi Hendrix scene so that's why I stayed away. The joke was on me. I was only fooling myself. Surprisingly, once I went back to the office, I didn't feel awkward about seeing Kathy. I was sure Jenny had something to do with that. I was actually happy to see her, and, as usual, she looked great. She asked me about a message that an attorney had left for me. I said he was my friend's brother-in-law and that he might be able to help Jimi with a legal matter. Bob Levine came into the room, and I dropped the subject. We greeted each other.

While I was standing next to Bob, Kathy asked me, "Why don't you come by sometime and see our apartment?" I had no intention of putting myself in that situation, but I had no willpower when it came to Kathy, so I said, "Sure. That would be great."

They were going to call a messenger service to bring paperwork to Jimi at the Electric Lady construction site. I offered to do it, saying I was going down there anyway, which was a lie. At the site, one of the construction workers led me into a recording studio that was being completed. Jimi was sitting on bags of concrete mix. I greeted him and handed him the envelope. He opened it.

"Vultures, fucking vultures," Jimi said, then started ranting. I was caught by surprise. This was not the Jimi I knew. Jimi was one of the most polite, kindest, soft-spoken, mild-mannered people I had ever met. I'd never seen him lose his temper or raise his voice.

"I've been spending a lot of money, but I've been making a lot of money. You know what Jeffery just told me? That I'm broke! That I don't have enough money to finance the studio and we have to fuckin' borrow from Reprise."

He tossed the papers on the ground and started pacing back and forth. "I did this one gig that was supposed to be for ten thousand, but I found out it was really for fifty thousand! You know what Noel told me? Jeffery has a bank in the Bahamas he set up where he sends money. There are going to be changes. I'm talking to your friend's lawyer and every lawyer I can find. I'm gonna straighten this shit out." He picked the papers up off the floor and left the building. I waited till he was gone.

Electric Lady was taking shape and starting to feel like a living room. John Storyk was doing an incredible job and was completely into Jimi's vision. Excitement was building because the studio was now becoming a reality. Jimi decided he wanted to start recording as soon as the construction noise was manageable.

I didn't hear from Jimi for a while after his rant. Then one day he called out of the blue. He started talking about the script again. He wanted to break free of the rock 'n' roll concert scene completely so he could focus on the kind of music he wanted to create. No more concert scene. No more crowds to please. No more circus act or costume show. Jimi said he was on the path to setting himself free. He told me he was planning to hire a Black attorney, Ken Hagood, to break Jeffery's stranglehold. He asked me to come over to his apartment.

By now Jimi had moved into his new apartment at 89 West Twelfth Street in Greenwich Village. It was November 1969, and he invited me over to see it. I was at the door of Jimi's apartment on West Twelfth Street, about to go in, when a black limo pulled up in front. The window rolled down, and Mike Jeffery said, "Get in." It wasn't a request. I wasn't in the limo more than a minute when Jeffery tore into me. He knew that I had suggested to Jimi that he get a lawyer.

I remember how cool, calm, and direct he was, almost threatening, jabbing his finger in the air at me and saying: "Do *not* interfere in my business. There are things going on you don't know about. You could get hurt, really hurt. I could shut your stupid-ass film down, and it will never get made, and I'll see to it that you and Hendrix never work with each other."

I tried to be upbeat when I told him that the project was going very well and that Jimi had great ideas to bring in other musicians. That turned out to be the wrong thing to say.

Jeffery was nearly screaming at me, "There will be no other fucking musicians! *Period!* Back off and don't get involved in something that's not part of your business."

I figured I'd better get out of this car. I didn't know where this was going.

"I'm going up to see Jimi," I said. "He's expecting me."

"No you're not, you're fucking leaving. I'm going up to see Jimi! Now get the fuck out!" he yelled.

I'm amazed he didn't physically throw me out of the car. I know he was still shouting after that, but I don't remember what he said. I just got out of the limo and grabbed the first cab that came by. I never told Jimi about it.

19

Miles Davis

About a week later, also November 1969, I stopped by the office. Jimi wasn't around; I learned that he was at his apartment, so I decided to give it another try and go see him, this time without a Michael Jeffery interruption. I knew very little about the building when I first visited, but as time went on, I learned a lot more. On this day, however, I was standing in the foyer of 59 West Twelfth Street trying to convince the doorman to announce me so I could go up. Jimi's apartment was on the eleventh floor. It would have been easier to find a parking space on a weekday in the neighborhood than it was trying to make this guy understand that I had a reason to be here. Ironically, as time went on and I came and went with great regularity, the doorman and I actually became friends; in fact, I even gave him a Christmas present that first year. Sadly, it turned out to be the only Christmas Jimi would have there; he would be dead before the next one.

When Jimi finally buzzed me up, I knocked on his apartment door. Jimi opened the door slightly and then hid behind it. It was odd behavior, and I never understood or asked why he did it. He usually had someone else open the door, but if he did it himself, he hid behind it, almost as if he didn't want anyone to know he was there. After a while, I was the one who let people in.

I was impressed the moment I walked into his apartment. Colette Mimram and Stella Douglas, who had accompanied him on his trip to Morocco a few months earlier, had decorated it in a Moroccan theme. The furniture had a rough-hewn look, intricate carvings, and mother-of-pearl and mosaic tile inlays. The curtains were made of dark, lush fabrics in rich colors, with intricate textures and busy patterns. There were also upholstered seats and ottomans covered in ornate velvets and silks. The entire environment was warm, exotic, mysterious, and inviting.

The new apartment also was refreshingly quiet, because none of the usual hangers-on knew that Jimi had found a new place. I knew that would change soon, and I was anxious to take advantage of the quiet time. That first day I visited, I brought plenty of notes and some script sides to read to Jimi. I was all about getting down to work.

"This is a really cool apartment," I said. Then: "I know you're busy and your asshole of a manager has booked you solid, but before you start touring, can we at least do one session and then I'll take it from there and work on it while you're off touring, or whatever you're going to be doing?"

"Yeah. Sometime. We'll pick up where we left off. Not today."

Jimi excused himself and headed to the back bedroom, telling me he was expecting a friend and to open the door when he showed up. He didn't tell me who the friend was. I think he did that on purpose. Although it hasn't been written about very much, Jimi had a great sense of humor.

Almost immediately there was a knock on the door. I went over and looked through the peephole. I couldn't believe who was on the other side! I quickly opened the door, not wanting to keep the person waiting. There stood Miles Davis, dressed outrageously, with large black shades wrapped around his head. I graciously invited him in, but Miles stood firm and almost growled at me. I told him that Jimi was in the back bedroom and invited him in. What did Miles do? He grabbed the door handle and slammed the door shut! I had no idea what was going on. *What the fuck had I done?*

I didn't know what to make of it. So I opened the door again and urged Miles to come in, so as not to create a scene in the hall.

Miles exploded. *"What's with these fucking white boys opening Jimi's door?"* he shouted, then yelled at me to go get Jimi immediately. And then he slammed the door in my face.

I rushed back to Jimi's bedroom and told him what had just happened.

He laughed and said, "Yeah, he's like that. You're not the first one; don't let it bother you." Then he headed to the apartment door, opened it, and let Miles in.

Miles made a comment about "white boys" again and warned Jimi if it were to happen again, he would leave. Jimi ignored the comment and led Miles to his back bedroom. Miles walked right by me as if I didn't exist. I stood awkwardly in the middle of the living room. All I could think of was Jimi's comment that Miles had done the same thing before to others.

Miles Davis was probably one of the most influential and acclaimed musicians in the history of jazz—and of twentieth-century music, for that matter. And here he was standing next to Jimi Hendrix, one of the biggest rock stars in the world. It seemed like an odd pairing. But beyond that, these guys were two of the coolest dudes around, and they were here together, talking.

Miles had a distinctly raspy voice, which added to his aura of coolness. I would later learn that his voice was the result of a throat operation he'd had about fourteen years before.

Both Miles and Jimi were ignoring me, but what I was hearing was worth it. I felt like the proverbial fly on the wall. They were talking about how Miles was thinking of playing the Fillmore East in New York sometime during the summer of 1970. Columbia Records, his label, wanted him to record a live album—and not just any live album but one that would capture him playing his new music for a new audience, a rock audience. It was Clive Davis who had instigated the event; he contacted Bill Graham, the man who created the rock concert hall revolution of the 1960s and 1970s. Miles Davis was starting to break out of his jazz roots, and Clive felt he was ready to capture new fans.

Even though I was privy to the information that Miles Davis was going to play the Fillmore East, I didn't act on it, and I missed the concert—which was pretty hard to do, because he did a four-night run there in the early summer of 1970. Miles was the greatest jazz trumpeter playing the leading rock venue in New York City, and Jimi was there. I wasn't. I've regretted that ever since.

Afterward a live double album was released, chronicling Miles' four-night run. It went on to become the standard for all popular music acts at the time. His band consisted of Chick Corea on electric keyboard, Keith Jarrett on organ,

Dave Holland switching back and forth between stand-up bass and electric bass guitar, Jack DeJohnette on drums, Airto Moreira on percussion, and a newcomer, Steve Grossman, on saxophone and flute. I know all this because I have the album. It cemented Miles Davis' reputation as being instrumental in the development of jazz, and his reputation as one of the top musicians of his era. With that performance, he was at the helm of changing the concept of jazz.

But on that November day in the apartment, Jimi came out and asked me to leave. No explanation given. I didn't need one. I never ran into Miles Davis at Jimi's apartment again.

I would learn later on that Miles and Jimi were friends. Kathy would tell me that when Jimi released his third Jimi Hendrix Experience album, Miles had just married a twenty-three-year-old woman named Betty Mabry, who was a big Jimi Hendrix fan. She introduced Miles to Jimi's music. Miles was blown away and from that point on wanted to meet Jimi. Kathy said that Miles was fascinated by everything about Jimi: his musical creations, the way he dressed, his freedom, his appeal, his flamboyance onstage, and most of all, the power of Jimi's music to draw young audiences, something Miles was missing. She assumed that because Jimi was a blues-based guitarist, Miles started listening to as many of the blue greats as he could, such as Muddy Waters, B. B. King, Robert Johnson, Willie Dixon, Buddy Guy, Howlin' Wolf, Lead Belly, Etta James, Paul Butterfield, even the Yardbirds and John Mayall & the Bluesbreakers. Miles absorbed them all. He was obsessed with trying to find a way to get that "voicing" into his music. Supposedly, after Jimi and Miles became friends, Miles started to use electric instruments in his music—first the bass guitar and then electric piano.

I have no idea how Jimi and Miles met. Jimi never told me, and there are so many different stories that I don't think anyone knows which are true and which aren't, but one thing is undisputable: Once they met, Miles and Jimi's friendship just grew. Dave Holland, Miles' bassist, was convinced that Jimi was influencing Miles, but I would come to learn that it was actually a two-way street.

Bitches Brew, a great Miles Davis record, was recorded in August 1969, right after the Woodstock Festival had taken place, and you could almost hear the Jimi Hendrix influences in the rhythms, the compositions, the instrumentation. The album featured a bass clarinet, two to three electric pianos, two drummers, all sorts of exotic percussion, and the amazing electric guitar of John McLaughlin, who many felt had the same intensity in guitar playing as Jimi did. However, the album divided Miles' fans and critics alike. One of the top jazz critics of the day said, "Miles Davis is the most brilliant sellout in the history of jazz." He also called Miles a traitor. And a nasty feud developed between Miles and fellow trumpeter Wynton Marsalis, who publicly criticized Miles' work with jazz fusion every chance he could, claiming it wasn't "true" jazz, that Miles was a sellout, a rock star wannabe.

Miles was unaffected. He knew he had to move away from the old jazz and into blues-rock—but to do more than that, to bring blues-rock and jazz together. And he did, with his jazz fusion.

I once heard that Miles was complaining to John McLaughlin that he had never seen Jimi play, so McLaughlin took Miles to see the documentary film *Monterey Pop*—which shows Jimi setting his guitar on fire after playing "Hey Joe." Miles was blown away. But as I said, it was really a two-way street. Miles also influenced Jimi musically and in other ways.

As I got to discuss ideas for music for our movie, it became evident that Jimi was growing very dissatisfied with the whole rock scene and with Mike Jeffery, who was insisting—no, more like demanding—that The Jimi Hendrix Experience stay together and continue touring. However, on the last Jimi Hendrix Experience album, *Electric Ladyland*, Jimi experimented a little with some new forms—with some Miles Davis–influenced jazz improvisations rather than just rock. It progressed a little further with Band of Gypsys, which featured avant-garde elements.

Not only did Jimi influence Miles, but Miles did the same for Jimi. It was because of Miles that Jimi decided against the three-piece Jimi Hendrix Experience for Woodstock, and instead created Gypsy Sun and Rainbows, which focused on rock-jazz-fusion instrumentation. Miles was influencing Jimi to experiment and push the limits of his own music style. Jimi was so taken by Miles, it seems, that he once dragged me out to Tower Records in NYC to buy a string of jazz albums and every Miles Davis album. Jimi was in love with Miles' *Kind of Blue* album.

Mike Jeffery noticed Jimi's lineup for his new band at Woodstock and was none too happy about it. He knew that Jimi was disenchanted with how The Jimi Hendrix Experience was playing the same old shit tour after tour, and that Jimi was experimenting because of Miles Davis' influence. Jeffery suspected, rightfully so, that Miles and Jimi had decided to put a band together and go into the recording studio and cut a record together.

They reached out to producer Alan Douglas, Jimi's friend, to set up the session, and then they started looking for musicians for their band. They decided to use Tony Williams on drums. Jimi wanted Paul McCartney to play bass and went so far as to send him a telegram, but unfortunately McCartney was tied up and couldn't do it. As they continued sourcing musicians for their band, the combination of Mike Jeffery's intense jealousy and suffocating control over Jimi, and Miles' out-and-out greed, got in the way. The day before they were to go into the studio to record some tracks of some of their collaborative compositions, Miles demanded a payment of $50,000. That was just the excuse Jeffery needed, and he killed the session. It was over before it even began. Alan Douglas was furious. He had gone through all of this trouble so that Miles and Jimi could record original music, and the plan collapsed.

Probably even more chilling is that Jimi's last concert performance was at the Isle of Wight Music Festival in August 1970, where Miles also played. There, Jimi and Miles, away from the clutches of Mike Jeffery, patched things up. They agreed to meet with arranger Gil Evans to record some of the compositions they'd created, but then on September 18, 1970, Jimi died of barbiturate-related asphyxiation. It has been said that Miles destroyed all traces of their original collaborations, never to play them or even discuss them again. It really makes you think—what if? Just imagine what that collaboration would have been like.

Perhaps the only time Jimi and Miles ever played together to create a piece of music was in Jimi's apartment, first for the concert promoter Terry, but it wasn't planned; it was an accident of fate. What Terry heard left him speechless—it was not unlike what Paul Butterfield had created for *Avril*. If only someone could have captured it.

Two hundred people attended Jimi's funeral in Seattle. Miles was asked to be a pallbearer. This was a big deal because Miles hated attending funerals. He hadn't even attended his own mother's funeral, but, for the first time, he made an exception for Jimi Hendrix. At the funeral, there was a jam session. Miles was asked to play. He refused.

After Jimi died, Miles searched for a guitar player who sounded like Jimi, but soon came to realize there was no one like Jimi. No guitar player existed who could play like Jimi. So he began to play his trumpet using the wah-wah pedal, which Jimi had used, trying very hard to sound like Jimi.

In 1992, the year after Miles Davis died, I was living and working in LA for an independent production company and was asked to interview a young actress. We met at a hotel bar and were talking about film things and where she could fit in, when I asked her what she was doing for work. She revealed that during the last year of Miles Davis' life, she had been his assistant and cared for him when no one else really had. Miles felt that everyone had deserted him. He was so appreciative of her and trusted her so much that when he passed away, he left it to her to catalogue and arrange for the sale of his art collection.

I became much more interested in her role handling that art collection, and what she was going to do with it, than in her role as an actress. We spent the remainder of the time talking about Miles Davis—what he had been like as a person, and his art. I was fascinated by her take on him and her stories about him. For some reason, I never revealed my brief encounter with Miles or Jimi's connection to him.

I never saw her again after that—and by the way, she was white.

20

Fillmore East, New Year's Eve 1970

It was late November 1969, and pressure was mounting on Jimi to deliver the album for the court settlement. With The Experience disbanded, Jimi was rehearsing Band of Gypsys, which had a date to play Fillmore East on New Year's Eve. The plan was to cut a live album of the concert.

Jimi invited me to stop by the studio, where he was rehearsing the new band. I went and saw Kathy there. She looked so great that I was mesmerized. There was absolutely nothing subtle about the way I was looking at her—leering is more like it. When she got up to go to the restroom, I followed her. We ended up having a mad, passionate make-out session in the ladies' room. I wouldn't exactly call it a romantic encounter, given the environment.

Again, I tried to tell her that it was definitely over between us. I felt too guilty whenever I was around Bob Levine; it was getting to the point where I couldn't do it. I liked him. He was a really good guy. In a way, I looked up to him. I started to tell her, but she took one long look at me and that went out the window. I couldn't get the words out. Kathy had me completely, body and soul.

I was excited about the Band of Gypsys concert. It was a snowy and sleet-filled New Year's Eve in New York City, but I didn't care about the weather. Neither did the throngs of people lined up outside of the Fillmore East, the famous rock concert venue on Second Avenue at Sixth Street. We were all there for Jimi Hendrix's New Year's Eve concert, his first ever at the Fillmore.

He couldn't have picked a better place. The Fillmore was a classic venue; few venues in rock history can match its legacy. It was the New York equivalent of Bill Graham's Fillmore West in San Francisco. Both were former movie theaters built in the 1920s, back in the day when movie theaters were beautiful Art Deco movie palaces. By today's standards, these theaters were huge, and they all had a balcony. The Fillmore East had 2,600 seats and the best kind of atmosphere to experience an astonishing array of live performances. Unlike the huge stadium concert venues that bands perform in now, it had perfect acoustics and an intimate feel. There was even a barrel full of free apples in the lobby for departing fans at the end of each concert.

It was only a concert venue for three years, but some of the greatest rock legends in the world played there: The Who, The Doors, Led Zeppelin, Janis Joplin, The Grateful Dead, Santana, Eric Clapton, The Beach Boys, John Lennon, Fleetwood Mac, to name a few. Interesting fact: The Fillmore East was one of the last venues Al Jolson performed live at, in 1950, during a promotional tour for his movie biopic *Jolson Sings Again*.

And, of course, Jimi Hendrix played there. Amazingly, the ticket prices were just three to five dollars, so I attended on a regular basis. Today it's a bank with a commemorative plaque on the outside identifying it as the site of the Fillmore East from 1968 to 1971. Jimi Hendrix is one of the names on the plaque.

On New Year's Eve 1969, the street outside the Fillmore was buzzing with people waiting to ring in the New Year with a concert by Jimi Hendrix and his Band of Gypsys. They were booked to play two shows that night, an early show and a late show.

Given that it was an all-Black band, it was a departure from what fans were used to, and many of them weren't prepared for it. It leaned more toward R&B and straight blues rather than the wildly diverse psych-rock that Jimi had become famous for. I was aware of this, and I didn't care. I had a pass to the concert from Jimi's office, so I just sailed through the lobby, past the ticket booth, and into the theater and took my seat—a good one.

There was a very festive party atmosphere inside the theater, not unlike at a Grateful Dead concert. Lots of joints were being passed around, and lots of brown bag wine and whiskey were quietly, and sometimes not so quietly, being shared. Jimi's engineer, Eddie Kramer, was in the house to record the shows for the live album. The Voices of East Harlem, a Gospel choir, opened for Band of Gypsys. The audience wasn't ready for this, but they were respectful and tolerated them, knowing that Jimi would soon be following.

However, they were completely unprepared for what followed. Even though I knew in advance Jimi was going to try something different, it wasn't what I expected. I found everything the band did interesting; however, the audience certainly didn't share my feelings.

Rather than perform the hits that everybody was expecting (and wanted), the group opted for a more, shall we say, adventurous excursion into the night. The set list included "Power of Soul," "Lover Man," "Hear My Train A-Comin'," "Them Changes," "Izabella," "Machine Gun," "Stop," "Ezy Ryder," "Bleeding Heart," "Earth Blues," and "Burning Desire," with Buddy Miles, not Jimi, doing most of the vocals. Buddy also was the one interacting with the audience by introducing each song and making small talk whenever he could. It was almost as if Jimi was just a side player. Jimi did play some new numbers, but the band did a lot of Buddy's material with Buddy singing.

The overwhelmingly white rock 'n' roll audience wasn't into it. I realized that whatever Jimi thought people liked and what they really wanted from him had nothing to do with reality. People started walking out. Those that stayed were calling out for things like "Purple Haze," "Hey Joe," and every other overplayed hit that Jimi Hendrix had come to be known for. Jimi ignored them.

The overall reception was lukewarm at best, and at times almost bordered on hostile rejection. I had a backstage pass, so once the show was over, I made my way through the departing and disgruntled throng of fans to the backstage area. Despite the swarm of hangers-on—the groupies and assorted bottom feeders that populated the cramped space—I was allowed back into Jimi's dressing room, along with just a couple of other people. Jimi briefly acknowledged me when I entered the dressing room, but he was involved in a heavy discussion with Buddy Miles and Billy Cox.

I decided there was nothing for me here. Just as I was about to leave, the dressing room door burst open and a wild-eyed Bill Graham blew into the room. He was furious! The veins were running through his temples like coaxial cables. I thought they were going to burst. I'd never met the man, had only seen pictures of him and an occasional TV interview. He was seething. Spit was flying from his mouth as he tore into Jimi.

"*What the fuck do you think you're doing out there?*" he screamed. He was not just yelling but actually screaming. Jimi, being as cool and laid back as usual, cracked a small smile and looked at Buddy as if to say, *What is this guy talking about?* But Graham wasn't finished with him. He was ranting, getting closer to Jimi's face. "People paid good money to hear you play, and you've got to give them what they want! And what they want is your fucking hits. All of them! *Got it? Do you hear me?* Then fucking answer me!"

"Everything is cool," Jimi said calmly. Even I couldn't believe how cool he was. "We're having a good time; they are having a good time. It was a good show."

Graham was having none of it. "People were walking out. That's not a good fucking show! That's a disaster! *Do you hear me?*" Now right up in Jimi's face, Graham repeated himself, emphasizing each word slowly and forcefully: "I said. Do. You. Hear. *Me?*"

Jimi kept his cool, saying, "I need to do what I need to do."

I had to get out of there; it was getting way out of hand. It looked as if Graham was going to have a heart attack. He was focused solely on Jimi. When Buddy saw me slink out of the room, he followed.

I was headed back out to watch the next show of the evening when Buddy caught up to me. "Here, take this," he said, slipping something into my hand. "You're going to enjoy this."

I would find out later that it was a psychedelic mushroom. If I had bothered to ask, I wouldn't have taken it, because I didn't do psychedelic drugs. They just weren't my thing. Wine, beer, and pot—that was me. But I didn't mind the fact that Buddy wanted me to be in a certain state of mind before the band played again. He handed me a bottle of champagne, and I swallowed the mushroom tab. As I walked away he said, "Just don't let it make you start thinking like a white person." We both laughed.

Graham's people had already cleared the house and brought the new ticket holders in for the midnight show. I sat in my seat, waiting for the drug to kick in, not really sure what to expect. I was nervous. About twenty minutes later, the house lights went down, and the Gospel choir performed. Still nothing drug-wise. I thought I was fine, then out of nowhere it hit me, just as Jimi came out with the band. The purple curtains on each side of the stage started turning to liquid, almost like paint melting, running down the side of the stage. The liquid was completely enveloping Jimi and the rest of the band in an ocean of purple foam and waves. Then they started playing. I don't know if I imagined it or it actually happened, but I think they were playing "Purple Haze," and here I was literally in a sort of psychedelic purple haze. I was trying to stay afloat in the "liquid." Nothing made sense to me.

Sitting a couple of rows in front of me was a gorgeous, angelic blonde. She had green eyes and a black tank top I think, and she was sensuously swaying and weaving and reacting to the music. Feeling the full effects of the drug by now,

I saw her as a hypersexualized goddess that I was literally breathing into my system. As she swayed to the music, the molecules around her body formed a kaleidoscopic chaos—colors bursting, glowing, and pulsating to the primal rhythms. I was entering an entirely new state of consciousness.

I tripped through much of the second show, which was great. It was a 180-degree departure from the first. Jimi sang more, played more, and did a lot of his usual shtick. The audience loved it. It took me a while to realize that Jimi altered his set, playing not only "Purple Haze" but "Foxy Lady" and "Voodoo Child," and others. It was a quintessential Jimi Hendrix performance; he jackknifed and sashayed like the onstage demon he was. And the crowd went insane.

After the house lights came on at three a.m., I started coming down. Wow. Of course, none of us had any way of realizing we had just lived a piece of history. Whatever I took, I don't regret it to this day, but I never did it again. I absorbed that music on an entirely different level. The audience seemed more than satisfied as we all trundled out into the cold to start 1970. A new decade. Jimi had been on fire. Whatever the reason, he had been feeling it and so had we. I was still in a bit of a daze as I hit the street, and I wandered home.

21

The Hotel Navarro

During this time, I was dating Jenny, the girl from the Playboy Club. I called the office to let them know that I had developed two rolls of film I'd taken of Jimi in the recording studio and wanted to drop them off. The person who answered (not Kathy) told me that Jimi was spending a few nights at the Hotel Navarro on Central Park South before his concert at Madison Square Garden. Jimi must've cleared the sharing of this info with me. I called Jenny and asked her to meet me there, adding that we could go to dinner afterward. I think she said yes because she was curious as to who this Jimi Hendrix person was.

Jimi was staying in a large two-bedroom suite. I had no problem getting past the front desk to go up to the room. Interestingly, there was no security.

I know Jimi had his share of beautiful women, but Jenny had something irresistible about her—a pinch of innocence, like Natalie Wood. More than that, she was beautiful in a classical sense—with long, silky jet back hair; milky white skin;

and striking features—but she was also a sexy, smart, self-assured woman with a great sense of humor.

Jimi looked caught off guard when he opened the door and saw the two of us standing there. I'm sure he thought she was a fan that I'd brought to introduce her to him so I could score some points with her. He had no idea how far from the truth that was. I introduced the two of them, and they politely shook hands. Then Jimi and I sat down in the living room, and Jenny pulled up a chair, facing us.

I showed Jimi the contact sheets, two of them with twenty-four pictures each. He remarked on a couple he liked on the first sheet, then handed it back to me and looked at the other. I handed Jenny the first contact sheet, and she looked at the pictures.

"Are you a musician?" she asked Jimi.

Jimi looked at me with a *WTF?* look on his face.

"Jimi, she doesn't know who you are," I told him. "Really. She's not into rock music, or jazz, or pop. She's a classically trained concert pianist, and she only has a classical record collection. That's her thing."

"And opera, too," added Jenny. "And what Jonathan said isn't entirely true. I do know some popular music artists, like The Beatles, Bob Dylan, Frank Sinatra—my parents listen to him. Oh, and Miles Davis. I've heard his music; it's as complex as some classical pieces."

Jimi chuckled, and almost under his breath said, "We all know Miles Davis, don't we?"

"Sorry. I'm sure you're very good," Jenny said. "I apologize that I don't know anything about you, but Jonathan didn't tell me anything. He doesn't talk about you. And I didn't really ask."

Jimi looked at me and laughed, but the fact that she didn't know who he was and that she didn't follow rock changed his whole demeanor. Now he was no longer the rock star but some guy trying to impress a girl. He assumed she must be into poetry, and he was right, so he got up and went into the bedroom and returned with a small carry-on suitcase. In it were pages and pages of handwritten poetry, written on different pieces of hotel stationery from around the U.S. and Europe, as well as on random scraps.

He picked one up and read it, almost shyly. He lifted a couple more from the suitcase, read them, and placed them on the coffee table in front of the couch.

Jenny looked at him and asked, "May I?"

Jimi nodded, and she took a couple out of the suitcase and read them to herself, then put them down and said to him, "This is really good."

He admitted that some were potential songs he was writing, but that he was considering writing a book of poetry someday and getting it published. Jenny read another one and encouraged him to do it someday.

Then Jenny said she also was an artist, and he went back into the other room and came out with a trunk. He placed it in the middle of the room and pulled out painting after painting of his. Before this, I'd never had a clue that he was a painter. (To this day, I have hanging on a wall in my apartment a framed Jimi Hendrix original watercolor painting.) I might as well not have been in the room; he directed everything to Jenny. It turned out she was an art collector but also had minored in art in college, while majoring in classical music.

The discussion between them went on for a while, until he got up and took two bottles of wine out of the hotel suite fridge. We opened both of them and started drinking, laughing, and talking. I don't remember how we got on the subject, but Jimi excitedly told us about his flat in London and why he considered it his first real apartment. He talked about living there with his British girlfriend (now ex-girlfriend), Kathy Etchingham, speaking fondly of her.

Jimi met Kathy Etchingham the day he arrived in London in 1966, and they became involved in a relationship that lasted over two and a half years. She was the inspiration for some of his songs, including "Gypsy Eyes" and "The Wind Cries Mary." Rumor has it she was "Foxy Lady." As Jimi had broken up with her earlier in the year, he wasn't that eager to get into any details. He just left it at that. I never spoke to him about her, so I really never knew much about their relationship other than that they had a lot of feelings as well as respect for each other. It was Kathy who'd found the apartment in London that they moved into together.

Listening to him, I could tell Jimi loved that place. It was on the top floor of an eighteenth-century house in London's Mayfair neighborhood. He had no neighbors, so he could play music as loud as he wanted. He talked about how he always had his acoustic guitar in the flat and revealed that he composed most of his songs on it, not on an electric guitar.

Jimi knew he could impress Jenny with this next piece of information, and he was right. His building was next to the house of the famous classical composer George Frideric Handel, who lived there from 1723 until his death in 1769. Jimi claimed that he'd seen Handel's ghost one night. He thought it was so cool to be living next to the home of a famous eighteenth-century classical composer. He said that when he found that out, he went to the local record store and bought all of Handel's records, and he played Handel's *Messiah* continuously. Jenny knew the piece intimately, having played it many times in piano recitals, as well as other classical pieces by Handel. She got into a discussion with Jimi about it and shared some obscure facts about Handel that she knew. Jimi ate it up.

Jimi said that when he was touring Europe in 1968, he would always return to London; he considered London and that apartment to be his base. It was tucked away on a cobblestone alley on Brook Street, and it's his only surviving home. It was filled with antiques and textiles; Jimi was heavily into both. He said that he was into Persian rugs and that he was always buying new ones until there wasn't any room left for yet another rug.

The two of them laughed about that because Jenny, too, was into Persian rugs and knew all about them. That led into a whole other discussion between the two of them about rare Persian rugs. I was not part of the conversation. I just sat closely by, drinking one glass of wine after another while listening to one of the world's top rock stars talking about decorating apartments. It was surreal. Something I learned that night, among other things, was that Jimi was obsessively neat, which he said was the result of his being in the Army. He laughed and said he even made his bed every day with hospital corners, like he'd learned to do in the Army.

Today, Jimi's London apartment and Handel's house next door are museums. Jimi's flat has been open to the public since February 2016; Jimi's sister Janie Hendrix was an honored guest at the opening.

Jimi told us about when he'd first started out playing the Chitlin' Circuit throughout the South, that segregation still existed in the United States but not in London. He felt totally accepted in London. It was a multicultural city, and he was accepted for his music. The Brits were color-blind. Black or white, it didn't matter; it was his talent and who he was as a musician that mattered.

As he was chatting with Jenny, Jimi, who was normally very shy, became increasingly at ease—very pleasant, laid back, and polite. Despite his rock star status and style of dress, there was nothing pretentious about him. He was just Jimi being Jimi, nothing more.

Jenny asked Jimi about his band, The Jimi Hendrix Experience, and was surprised to hear it had only three members, including himself. He told her how it had been formed in London. Now he directed part of the discussion toward me because I knew Mitch, the drummer. He told me something I didn't know: that originally he and Chas Chandler had been deciding whether to choose Mitch or Aynsley Dunbar as the drummer, and they couldn't. So Chas tossed a coin, and Mitch won. That's how a laid-back British jazz drummer named Mitch Mitchell became the drummer for one of the biggest rock bands of the time, The Jimi Hendrix Experience.

Mitch was one of the most iconic psychedelic-blues-rock drummers of all time. Jimi spoke respectfully of Mitch, almost glowingly. He said that Mitch was the perfect drummer for the band, because he had an uncanny ability to play the perfect rhythms for whatever Jimi threw at him, and it was all Mitch, because there weren't any other drummers out there that Mitch could lean on for inspiration. Jimi's music was unique; no one else was creating anything like it. In a sense, Mitch became a pioneer. Noel Redding quit The Jimi Hendrix

Experience in 1969, but Mitch stayed with Jimi right up until Jimi's death in September 1970.

Jimi stayed on the subject of music and asked Jenny about classical music, her training as a concert pianist, her playing of Handel's compositions, and about other classical musicians. She, in turn, asked Jimi about his music. I could see Jimi was touched, because there was someone who before tonight hadn't known anything about him asking sincere questions, because she was genuinely curious and wanted to know about him and his music. It was real; there was nothing fake about her. She wasn't a groupie, and she wasn't after anything; she just found him to be fascinating, intelligent, delightful, and an artist. Jimi loved it. It was two artists getting to know one another.

The more wine we drank, the more questions were asked and the more in depth we got. I even started asking Jimi questions. I asked how he'd started playing the guitar—probably everyone knows this, but I didn't. His father bought him his first guitar, but it didn't have strings; those came in a separate package. Plus, it was a right-handed guitar, and Jimi was left-handed. He didn't know how to string a guitar, but he had a record by Duane Eddy, a rock 'n' roll guitarist of the late 1950s who was famous for creating the twangy guitar sound. The cover art was a large picture of Duane Eddy sitting with a guitar in his lap, prominently displayed facing the camera. Jimi said he took a magnifying glass and studied the thickness of each string and copied it, and that's how he strung his first guitar. However, photographs are flipped, so Jimi strung the guitar backward. Plus, Jimi was left-handed, so he started to learn how to play the right-handed guitar upside down. He didn't say it, but I wondered if that's how he'd created his unique style and sound. He also said that he never sang in the beginning; he was basically the guitar player in various bands.

I asked why he'd started singing if he wanted to just play the guitar, and he laughed and said that Linda Keith had convinced him. Jimi's idol was Bob Dylan, as I've mentioned, and Linda apparently said that Jimi's singing couldn't be worse than Dylan's.

"Who's Linda Keith?" Jenny asked.

I knew a little something about her, that she was a beautiful twenty-year-old English *Vogue* model who was Keith Richards' girlfriend. (Jimi had to tell Jenny who Keith Richards was.) Linda walked into a nightclub in New York City one night where Jimi was playing guitar in a not-so-great band. He told us he had been performing under the name Jimmy James. We all laughed at that one. Well, according to Jimi, she stayed, sat at the bar, and when the set was over, she invited him to have a drink with her. She was so beautiful and had such a cool British accent that he immediately said yes.

He was impressed that she knew he played his right-handed guitar left-handed, upside down, and strung backward. The more they talked, the more they discovered they both had a love for the blues. She admitted to Jimi that she was a blues fanatic. So was Jimi. She revealed that she was the girlfriend of Rolling Stones guitarist Keith Richards and had been with him for the past three years. She told Jimi that she'd never heard anyone play the guitar like he did, and that she'd like to help him.

He told her, "I sacrifice part of my soul every time I play."

As their friendship grew, Linda made Jimi start performing as Jimi Hendrix. She also encouraged him to sing, despite his concerns about his voice and his lack of confidence. She brought up the Bob Dylan comparison. And he pointed out to Jenny and me that he owed her in many ways, but a very important thing she did for him was that she got ahold of a promotional record by Tim Rose called "Hey Joe."

Jimi couldn't say enough good things about her. When she heard him play, she couldn't believe that nobody had grabbed him to manage him. She told Andrew Oldham, the manager of The Rolling Stones, that Jimi was astonishing, the best guitar player she'd ever heard—that he had a great stage presence and unparalleled skill on the guitar. And yet nobody was jumping up and down to sign him, so Linda made it her mission to introduce Jimi Hendrix to the world, realizing it wasn't going to be easy. Jimi was virtually unknown.

Jimi said that Linda tried to get Keith Richards to listen to him, but Richards wasn't too happy that his girlfriend was hanging out with another musician, even though nothing was going on between them; they were genuinely friends. So Linda invited Oldham to hear Jimi play. Oldham wasn't impressed. Jimi commented that it was probably because Oldham had heard the rumors from Keith Richards that Linda was hanging out with Jimi, and Oldham didn't want to offend Richards. Oldham said he wasn't interested.

"Maybe it was because she lent me Keith's guitar without telling him," Jimi said. "I don't blame him. I would have been pissed, too."

The guitar in question was a white Fender Stratocaster, the guitar that would become forever associated with Jimi. He said that Richie Havens, a folk icon at the time, heard him play and befriended him, and that it was Havens who had recommended that Jimi play Cafe Wha?, because Richie and Bob Dylan had both played at the club and it was a great venue.

Coincidentally, years later Richie Havens and I would become friends, as I mentioned earlier, and I spent many a night in Woodstock, where he lived, hanging out with him and members of the community, drinking, smoking, philosophizing, and having fun. I never knew Richie's connection to Jimi, and he never knew mine. I never thought to ask him.

Jimi's performance at Cafe Wha?—which happened indirectly because of Richie Havens and directly because of Linda Keith, because it was Linda who invited the former Animals bassist turned artist manager, Chas Chandler, to come to see Jimi perform—turned his whole life around. Chas came not at night but midafternoon on a bright sunny day when the club was empty. I've been to Cafe Wha? and once you enter, you descend a couple of flights of stairs as if you're entering a subway station. Then you come upon a cave-like room with a small stage in the middle against the wall. Jimi said he did a version of "Hey Joe" for Chas, and the rest is history.

"What happened to Linda?" I asked him.

"She's around, but we lost touch. She lives in London."

I asked him if Linda was the "Foxy Lady" in his song. He said no. I could tell by the look on Jenny's face that she didn't know what I was talking about. I turned to her and said, "One of Jimi's most famous songs."

"Oh," is all she said.

I asked him if there was an actual lady behind the song. He didn't answer me directly but said that Kathy Etchingham maybe was "Foxy Lady", but used the word "maybe", and then said that Lithofayne Pridgon had inspired many of the songs on the *Electric Ladyland* album, alluding to her being the inspiration for "Foxy Lady." I loved her name, Lithofayne. I thought it was the coolest name.

I'd never met Lithofayne, but I'd heard about her. She was even signed to Atlantic Records at one time for an album that was recorded, but it was never released. I don't know why. She knew Jimi from his days as a struggling musician in Harlem in 1963 and was connected with him till his death in 1970.

Lithofayne must have had quite an influence on Jimi. An artist doesn't write a song, or several songs in her case, unless he or she has a real connection with that person. A number of cuts on *Are You Experienced* seem to have been written with her in mind. Jimi didn't admit it that night, but people around him would tell me there was real love between the two of them. Everybody in Harlem knew them as a couple at one time.

Somehow the conversation got back around to Jimi's father, Al Hendrix. Jimi spoke briefly about him. He shared how when Jimi was a boy, his dad had torn his clothes because he didn't like the type of clothes Jimi wore and had cut Jimi's hair because he didn't like it. But Jimi also defended his father's decision to give Jimi's brother and two sisters over to child services. Jimi's justification was that "times were hard. I guess he had to. He was struggling at the time."

He refused to elaborate, and the conversation switched back to guitars. Jimi said that as a kid he'd wanted a guitar so bad that he started playing guitar on a broom and even on a one-stringed ukulele. Seeing this, his father finally got Jimi a guitar when he was twelve. Jimi taught himself how to play, and he loved the blues. He learned blues songs from B. B. King and Muddy Waters records; they were his teachers. When I asked him how he'd come up with playing the guitar behind his back, between his legs, and over his head, he said he hadn't. All he'd done was copy other great blues guitarists before him who'd done the same thing, only most people didn't know that; they thought it was original to him.

He didn't want to talk about his father anymore. Jenny told him about her parents and the whole nudist thing, and I told him how I'd been blindsided, and he loved it. We just cracked up at each other's expense. We also cracked up when Jenny said as a kid she'd always run around the house without any clothes (sometimes outside, too), and people called her "Nudie"—a nickname she quickly dropped when she got to high school. Jimi revealed that when he was growing up, he'd been known as "Buster." We lost it over that one, but when Jenny asked him, "What about your mother? Was she into music?" Jimi got very quiet.

After Jimi had been staring into space for a few minutes, Jenny apologized for asking, but Jimi said it was okay. Jimi talked about his parents and growing up in Seattle. We could see that he idealized his mother. She was like an angel to him. She was his link to the Cherokee heritage he was so proud of. Talking about his mother was completely out of character for Jimi. Maybe it was the way Jenny asked the question, with all her innocence and wide-eyed enthusiasm. Jimi said, without any bitterness or judgment, "I've never seen my mother's grave. Never." It was sad the way he said it.

Jimi's mother's name was Lucille Jeter. She divorced his father, and Jimi's father gained custody of both Jimi and his brother, Leon. His mother had had a serious drinking problem. She got remarried, to a longshoreman who was thirty years older. She wasn't happy, and she drank to the point that she was hospitalized, twice, with cirrhosis of the liver. In early 1958, when Jimi was a teenager, she was found lying in an alley beside a tavern and was back in the hospital again with hepatitis. Soon afterward, in February 1958, she died of a ruptured spleen. She was only thirty-two. Jimi worshipped his mother.

Jimi said "Castles Made of Sand" was inspired by his mother and her escaping the toxic relationship she'd had with his father. Jimi seemed to be unhappy with his father for not taking better care of his mother, but despite that, Jimi loved his father. There was a bond between the two of them.

Jimi then quickly changed the subject, and he and Jenny danced from topic to topic: growing up in an ethnically mixed Seattle neighborhood where it was cool to be any color, and how that made him believe people are raceless; having friends to hang with who were not in the music business (Deering, Colette, and Stella). We touched on religion after Jenny commented that she had been brought up in a strict religious environment and had broken loose as soon as she got to college. Jimi said he'd been brought up as a Christian, but he considered himself a spiritual person, not a religious one. He was especially interested in Eastern religions and philosophies. Jimi was excited about the possibility of starting a new band and expanding his musical horizons. The only thing he said about that was that he was talking to Miles Davis.

Unsurprisingly, the discussion eventually led to Bob Dylan. Even though Jimi idolized Dylan, the two of them couldn't have been more different. It didn't matter; Jimi was a Bob Dylan disciple. Jimi followed Dylan up to Woodstock just to be around him, for God's sake. Dylan proved to Jimi that you could be an artist and a poet in popular music and be able to be your own man. Jimi credited Dylan for his growing as a songwriter instead of just being a guitar phenomenon, which he never considered himself to be, anyway. Jimi felt that Billy Gibbons of ZZ Top was a better guitar player than himself.

Dylan was the magic sauce, and anything connected with Dylan was gold. The way Jimi was talking, you'd think he was a friend of Dylan's, but he said he'd met Dylan only once, and that was a brief accidental run-in at Kettle of Fish in the Village. It was obvious that Jimi was obsessed with Dylan; in fact, one of Jimi's biggest hits, "All Along the Watchtower," was a cover of a Bob Dylan song, only Jimi made it his own. He completely transformed it. It's been said that when Dylan heard it, he felt so overwhelmed by what Jimi had done with it that from that point on, Dylan all but regarded it as a Jimi Hendrix song.

Jimi said that the inspiration for his version of the song had been the contemptuous and unhappy relationship he was having with Michael Jeffery, who was forcing Chas Chandler out of the picture so he (Jeffery) could have complete control over Jimi. We explained to Jenny as little as possible about who Jeffery and Chas were. Jimi didn't want to talk about it.

Since Jenny had never seen Jimi perform and didn't know of Jimi's reputation, she didn't know what he meant when he said he was tired of audiences who expected a "wild man" act. It confused her that such a statement was coming from the low-key, soft-spoken, laid-back, polite man sitting across from her. Jimi didn't bother to explain it, but I knew what he meant.

Then Jenny brought up the war in Vietnam—not surprisingly, because it was on everybody's mind then. It was the most unpopular war in American history. By now I knew Jimi's feelings, so I didn't want to comment. Jimi said he hated communism and supported the war but was now becoming more critical of it; he also felt that we must do whatever possible to support the soldiers. Jimi was all about the soldiers. That's what he cared about. He really didn't consider himself part of the music counterculture that was so outspoken against the war, and yet in a few days he would be performing at Madison Square Garden as part of a concert for peace. I don't know if there is such a thing as a radical conservative, but I would almost call Jimi one.

We said, debated, analyzed, picked apart, discussed, and revealed so much more, but after five hours, I was so wasted that I don't remember any of it.

The more Jenny and Jimi communicated, the more they related to each other. Even though I became a little jealous, it was exciting to watch. The entire time I'd known him and been around him, we'd never connected the way he did with Jenny. He was not a rock star to her, as I've said. He was an artist and a fascinating human being with enormous talent. And to him, she was a girl from another planet—a throwback who didn't know who he was and didn't care. She was curious and eager to learn more about his art and to share hers. She related to him as a person, not a rock god. I'd never experienced anything like this before, and never have since.

Because of Jenny, I learned new things about Jimi. He wasn't that forthcoming. He was more reserved and shyer than I thought, was entertaining and funny but also guarded about his feelings. That night, however, struck a chord. And to think, it hadn't been planned; it was all because I had pictures to show him. But I firmly believe that if Jenny hadn't decided to go with me, I would have probably just dropped off the pictures and left. Nothing like what happened would have happened.

This was the most important time I ever spent with Jimi, far surpassing the rare writing sessions and everything else I'd ever experienced with him. I can clearly picture him in my mind. I can picture the hotel. I can picture Jenny. I can picture the artwork, the poems. It was the only time he spoke about some of the things he told us about—his mother, for one.

After that night, he never again mentioned the time the three of us had spent together or anything we'd discussed. It was like an unwritten understanding that we were never to bring it up. So we didn't.

The visit to the hotel at nine p.m. to quickly drop off some contact sheets continued until seven o'clock the next morning. I was so wiped out when I left. The two of them were so pumped, their adrenaline still rushing, that they kept going. As I left, I somehow knew it was over between me and Jenny.

I often think of that night, how it had been totally un-planned, a fluke. I only wish I hadn't gotten so wasted, because I would love to be able to remember every little thing that was said. It was the most intimate time I ever had with Jimi, and probably with Jenny. The poetry I read, the paintings I saw, the explanations and revelations I heard, the way the night came together and then unfolded—unplanned, honest, no games—meant that the interaction between us had been real. I learned about Jimi Hendrix the person, the man behind the superstar facade, the musician, the poet, the artist. He had a great sense of humor, which only those around him had the opportunity to experience and enjoy.

The image in the press of Jimi as a drug-crazed wild man was the polar opposite of who he really was. Sure, we all took drugs then—it was the '60s; that's what everyone did—but the Jimi I had the privilege of knowing was only an occasional participant. He mostly shunned hard drugs; they weren't his thing. As he once said to me—and I still can hear his voice in my head: "The only drug I need is music. My music is my drug of choice...yesterday, today, and tomorrow. That's what gets me high."

Three days later, Jenny called me to thank me for the incredible introduction to Jimi and added that she'd decided it was not going to work between us. We ran in totally different circles, she said, and as much as she loved meeting Jimi, that wasn't her world or her lifestyle. It was mine, so I should embrace it, but she didn't want anything to do with it. That was the last time I ever spoke to Jenny. I never saw her again. She moved out of New York.

22

Madison Square Garden

A few days after the New Year's Eve concerts at the Fillmore, I went over to Jimi's apartment on West Twelfth Street. The plan was for us to work on *Avril* and make up some of the lost time on the script and soundtrack.

He asked me what I thought of the show.

"I really enjoyed it," I told him. "Both sets I saw were terrific, and I don't think Bill Graham knows what he's talking about."

Jimi laughed and kept pressing. "What do you think of the band? How good was Buddy Miles as a vocalist and as an emcee?"

I told him that Buddy had been very solid. He had a good presence, could definitely sing his ass off, and also was good with the crowd. Had a good sense of style and what it took to keep everybody engaged.

"Are we better than Cream or Mountain?"

"I mean, come on," I said. "Listen, you are the guy that makes the difference. There's nobody else like you. I wouldn't compare you to those bands because you are unique. Anything that you do is going to be special and automatically better."

I also told him my honest opinion about the audience's not being totally into the first show. I'd really liked the music, but I wasn't sure that they were ready for all of the new stuff.

"The second show," I told him, "I thought was totally unforgettable and amazing. However, thanks to the mushroom or whatever it was that Buddy gave me, I wasn't actually present all the time."

Jimi laughed and said, "You can still appreciate the music on acid. It's just a different experience."

He started talking about the music scene in general and the pressure that Bill Graham and Mike Jeffery were putting on him. It was a bit of a tangent actually.

"These guys need to let artists do what they're going to do," he said. "They're not the ones getting up there onstage and expressing themselves performing and being vulnerable. They just collect the money. It's no personal loss to them if an artist gets up there and takes a risk. It may just be a financial loss, and that's all they care about. I'm getting sick and tired of those guys and others expecting me to get up there and be like a trained monkey at the circus. They promote all the wrong shit. Like my clothes. They get people to come to see me for what I'm wearing and not the music."

He went on to complain about how Mike Jeffery was manipulating him and taking advantage of him, then repeated: "I'm getting sick of it."

I appreciated knowing where Jimi was coming from. It seemed like we had become friends. That day at his new apartment, I was ready to get cranking and really make some serious progress on the script. But his head was in a different space.

He just wanted to talk and get some things off his chest. I wish we could've done both, but with Jimi you had to just flow with his mood and timing. I knew we would get to it eventually; he just had to be in the right frame of mind.

Despite how excited Jimi was about Band of Gypsys, their fate was about to be determined by the ever-present Mike Jeffery, who had decided that enough was enough. Band of Gypsys was not commercial enough to produce the financial results that he was interested in, and so he summarily fired Buddy Miles. I ran into Billy Cox one day, and he said to me, "I'm getting my ass out of town before Jeffery can fire me as well. I'm not going to be humiliated like Buddy was."

I went back over to Jimi's apartment one day, and he was raging. I mean, he rarely showed emotional outbursts, but he was really upset.

"I can't believe what Jeffery has done now. He pulled a total power play by signing contracts with Mitch and Noel," he said. "How can he do that?"

It was stunning to me that Jeffery could be so cavalier as to overrule, or at least attempt to overrule, the creative desires of his client. But more and more, that just seemed to be his MO. Clearly, Jeffery saw dollar signs in front of a new Jimi Hendrix Experience tour, which is why Mitch and Noel were back in the fold. That's not what Jimi wanted to do at that point, but it didn't matter. I was curious how this whole thing was going to play out. There didn't seem to be anything but an ugly conclusion possible.

But Band of Gypsys wasn't completely dead yet. One last show was set to happen, and it became one of the most infamous moments in Jimi's career. How it all shook out still remains a mystery in many ways. But I was there. I saw it.

It was January 28, 1970. Jimi had already conquered Madison Square Garden the year before, but the mood of this booking was going to be slightly different. Jimi complained to people at the office a few days before the show that it was going to be like playing the Roman Coliseum.

The concert was billed as the Winter Festival for Peace and was going to feature, among others, Harry Belafonte; Blood Sweat & Tears; Judy Collins; Peter, Paul and Mary; the Rascals; and Jimi Hendrix and his Band of Gypsys. It was a fundraising event held eighteen months before the concert for Bangladesh, making it one of the first times that major performers donated their performances to benefit a specific political agenda. Sid Bernstein and Peter Yarrow organized the event. Sid was the promoter who had first brought The Beatles to America and was well loved by many performers for his antiwar stance. All of the monies from the show were to be donated to the Vietnam moratorium effort.

The one-night festival was to run from eight p.m. to one a.m., and I did not want to miss it. I had a chance to go backstage, but I didn't. I'd heard it was like a zoo back there. I'd heard that Mick Jagger was hanging out with several other rock luminaries there, not to perform but just to observe what was going on.

I took my seat and waited for the concert to start. Once it did, I found the show to be slow-paced, not really exciting. The performances were just okay, and things were running seriously behind. Finally, around three a.m., Jimi and his Band of Gypsys came out, and I could tell at once that something was off. He wasn't focused. I don't remember what they started off with, but it was basically a ten-minute jam, then the band took a brief break.

When they came back, they kicked into "Earth Blues," and Jimi played one of his trademark cosmic solos. Maybe he was getting it together. But then he seemed incoherent. "That's what happened when Earth fucks with space," he muttered before sitting down onstage. "Never forget that." Then he left the stage. And the audience waited.

A few minutes went by, and Buddy Miles took the microphone and said, "It seems as though we're not quite getting it together, so just give us a little more time, because it has been hard. Just bear with us for a few minutes and we'll try to get something together.... Like I said, we're having trouble...." But it was over after just twenty-three minutes. They never came back onstage. It was sad to watch this. Just two and a half years earlier, at Monterey Pop, Jimi had changed the world. But the man who was up there on this night did not even approach the iconic gypsy of Monterey.

The New Year's Eve shows at the Fillmore East were wonderful. Jimi was at the top of his game, Bill Graham's thoughts notwithstanding, and Band of Gypsys looked to be his next big musical chapter. But this was just awful. I'd never seen Jimi so out of it. It wasn't like him to fuck up the show like that.

A few days after the show, Jimi described the night to *Rolling Stone*'s John Burks. "It's like the end of the beginning or something," he explained. "I figure that Madison Square Garden is like the end of a big, long fairy tale. Which is great. I think it's like the best ending I could possibly have come up with. The Band of Gypsys were out of sight as far as I'm concerned. It was just going through head changes is what it was. I couldn't really tell. I was very tired. You know, sometimes there's a lot of things that add up in your head about this or that, and they might hit you at a very peculiar time, which happened to be at a peace rally. Here I'd been fighting the biggest war I ever fought. In my life. Inside, you know? And like that wasn't the place to do it."

I was eager to get back to the office the next day so I could perhaps find out what was going on. I knew I wouldn't be speaking to Jimi for a few days. Not after that night. I knew Jeffery did not want that band to continue. But would he have gone so far as to sabotage the performance? It was hard to avoid having that thought get lodged in my brain. And evidently somebody had sabotaged the performance, because unbeknown to Jimi, he had been dosed with some acid. Buddy Miles said Mike Jeffery had done it.

23

Summer of Touring

I stopped into the office one day in the summer of 1970 to see Kathy and catch up on where Jimi was in the world. For most of the summer, he was out on the Cry of Love tour. Billy Cox was on bass, and Experience drummer Mitch Mitchell was back on board. The band didn't have an official name, but they were billed as The Jimi Hendrix Experience in many places that they were playing. I had been seeing Jimi intermittently throughout the tour, because there would be gaps during the week, thus allowing him to come back to New York to work on his new album and other projects. I had given up on going any further with the script, so I just focused on photography and taking pictures when I was around him. But he was hard to track down during this time, and I thought maybe Kathy could help me.

Seeing Kathy, regardless of the circumstances, always gave me a rush. I could picture her in so many other provocative situations outside of the office, but on this day, I was fairly focused.

"What's up with Jimi?" I asked her casually. "Is he reach-able? When is he back?"

The look she gave me communicated that something was wrong. "He played in Seattle last night, and I guess things didn't go well," she said. "What should have been a nice home-coming turned into a mess."

I asked her to explain, and she told me that in addition to lots of rain at the outdoor baseball stadium where he'd per-formed, he had become agitated by the crowd and literally told them to fuck off multiple times. That wasn't like Jimi. He might have a bad night, but the idea of him going after the audience like that was out of character, especially in his hometown. Kathy went on to explain that he had been visiting his father. They got into an argument, and he'd brought some of that tension to the show. Evidently Jimi had called her after the show.

She told me that sometime in the middle of the night after the concert, Jimi, along with his cousin and a few family friends, started driving around Seattle, visiting some of his old boyhood landmarks, including the hospital where he had been born, the housing project where he had lived, his high school, and another former family home. That was interesting. What had made him so nostalgic suddenly? I didn't know what to make of any of this but thought maybe the Hotel Navarro night with Jenny.

Kathy was packing some things up in a bag as she was talking to me. She said, "I'm heading out to Maui right now. That's where the band is headed to put on a show, and then we'll be back in just a couple of days."

I had no way of knowing at this point that Jimi was only two months away from dying. But things were starting to feel a little bit desperate and unpredictable even for him. I knew he would be busy once he got back into town, with the opening of his studio, Electric Ladyland, about to happen.

I'll admit I was curious about why she was heading off to see him. I mean, I know she did a lot for him in the role of personal assistant, but it did seem slightly unusual for her to be heading off to meet him in Hawaii. Maybe he just needed to see her. Maybe it was a romantic tryst. Obviously, more important things than just a random visit were going on here. Besides, if anybody understood Jimi, it was Kathy.

The concert in Maui that Kathy was going off to see was filmed, and the footage was eventually released as part of a movie called *Rainbow Bridge*. I saw *Rainbow Bridge* at an arthouse theater on Eighth Avenue and Eighteenth Street in New York soon after Jimi died. To this day, I remember one piece of music he played in the film—a beautiful haunting instrumental ballad. In 2022, a fascinating documentary produced by Janie Hendrix and John McDermott called *Experience Hendrix*, about the concert, was released. The performances are riveting, the setting is beautiful, and the crowd size was quite intimate. As it turned out, it would be the last performance Jimi would ever give in the United States.

24

Launch Party: Electric Lady Studios

Limos were dropping off luminaries, record executives, musicians, models, artists, and stoners in front of a door sporting a large poster with the Electric Lady logo announcing: "Grand Opening—by invitation only." On August 26, 1970, Electric Lady Studios was launched with a lavish party for Jimi's fellow musicians and friends in what some referred to as Jimi's psychedelic studio lair.

After arriving, I walked down the stairs to the subterranean level, where the party was in full swing. Billy Cox, Buddy Miles, and Mitch Mitchell were there. Noel Redding had no intention of showing up and didn't. I got to talk to Buddy until an attractive, well-dressed magazine reporter pulled him away. I didn't blame him. Also mingling with the guests were Deering Howe and Stella Douglas. I knew it was a matter of time before Devon Wilson showed up. Jimi's musician guests included Eric Clapton, Steve Winwood, and Ron Wood.

I also noticed many executives from Warner Bros. Records. As I made small talk with one of them, he made it clear that they felt they were responsible for saving the studio, because the label had floated a $300,000 loan to complete construction. I saw engineer Eddie Kramer, and I wanted to talk to him, having never really had the chance. But I didn't; I got distracted.

As I mentioned earlier, the studio had been constructed specifically for Jimi with his tastes in mind. It had round windows, and there was a machine that generated ambient lighting in a myriad of colors. It was designed to have a relaxing feel to encourage his creativity, but it also provided a professional recording studio atmosphere. Jimi had envisioned an artistically free environment. With Jimi's vision as a guide, John Storyk created two recording studios, Studio A and Studio B. Jimi had directed Storyk to make the design very soft. He wanted lights to change and wanted things to be soft and curvy. He told Storyk that he wanted the base to be white and then he wanted the lights to be able to change it. Eddie Kramer put it best. He said everything had to be just right for a facility that had been "designed and built for Jimi with his vision in mind. It was a great vibe for Jimi to work in. He was so proud of it. This was something he had created with his hard work and his money and his efforts on the road and his sales of his albums. This was his home." It was truly the house that Jimi built.

Before Electric Lady existed, Jimi used to complain to anyone willing to listen that recording albums was usually difficult, because the recording sessions often were split between London's Olympic Studios and New York's Record Plant; and even that wasn't consistent, because sessions were regularly interrupted by touring commitments. It was no secret that Jimi was frequently frustrated by trying to get the right sound, the right music. As I've said several times by now, his perfectionism coupled with his never-ending fascination with sonic experimentation drove Noel to quit the band. But it was more than just that. Many times Jimi would show up at Record Plant with three, four, or even eight groupies and other hangers-on, and it would turn into a party atmosphere rather than a working recording session. I never saw this happen, but then again, I wasn't around that much during the recording sessions—fewer than half a dozen times.

"That was it. We got it," Noel would say while recording. Jimi would answer, "No, no, no," and go on to record another and another and another. Finally, Noel would just throw his hands up and leave.

It also frustrated the hell out of Chas Chandler, probably Jimi's most trusted ally; studio fees for the recording sessions were astronomical because of Jimi's obsession with getting each note right. Chas had come from the hit-and-run school of recording, and Jimi ended up alienating him with the combination of the studio party atmosphere and the dozens of takes Jimi would insist upon. So Chas eventually quit, too.

The fact that everyone was there on that hot August night for the opening must have been something of a miracle to Mike Jeffery, the Warner label execs, Eddie Kramer, and John Storyk. I don't think anyone at the launch party had any idea that construction had taken double the time and more than double the expected money.

According to Jeffery, the final cost ended up being a million dollars (equivalent to over $7.5 million today).

Devon was there, as I'd predicted. She was in one of the recording studios complete with messy hair, drooping eyelids, and a gray complexion. Devon was on a tear about something but thankfully couldn't be heard through the soundproof glass. I saw Jimi nodding to partygoers who said hello, but he seemed oblivious behind a mask of calm.

I wandered around the studio, which was set up with food. Not paying attention, I picked up an hors d'oeuvre. An attractive model type behind me remarked, "Is that really raw fish? Yuck!" I realized then that I was holding a piece of sushi, which back then was not as well-known as it is today. I was even surprised that it was there. I ate it anyway.

Then I heard a familiar voice say, "You better be more careful what you put in your mouth." I turned around and it was Kathy, dressed beautifully, walking by. She was on the arm of Bob Levine, and the two, chatting, headed up the stairs. Looking around, I was surprised not to see Colette Mimram there. I decided to head up the stairs myself and go out and get some fresh air.

Sitting near the top of the stairs at street level were Jimi and the singer Patti Smith, engaged in what appeared to be a deep conversation. Sometime later, I would learn that she had told Jimi that she was too chicken to join the party, and that Jimi admitted to her that contrary to what people might think, he was shy, and parties made him nervous. That was truly the Jimi his adoring public never had a clue about.

Soon there was commotion in Studio A. Jimi went to investigate and saw Devon and others throwing food at each other. Jimi's eyes narrowed in disgust. He must have realized the food fight was desecrating his "living room." Calling Devon a junkie, a very upset Jimi stormed up the stairs and out the front door.

Devon yelled after him, "You know I'm going to London, don't you?"

I had no idea where Jimi took off to, but I ran into Buddy, who told me that Jimi was going back to his apartment on Twelfth Street and that Buddy and a few of Jimi's "real friends" were going there, too. I decided to join them.

The launch party for Electric Lady Studios was meant to celebrate a high-tech facility that set a new standard for recording studios. I didn't know it then, but instead it ended up as a farewell event for Jimi Hendrix.

I walked over to West Twelfth Street, which was less than ten minutes from Electric Lady. I had no trouble getting into the building; by now the doorman and I had become friends. I don't remember who let me in—I think it was Mitch—but I noticed that there weren't many people there. It was more of a gathering than a party, which I'm sure was the way Jimi wanted it.

Jimi seemed to be recovered from his angry mood and was calm. I went into the kitchen and poured a glass of red wine, walked back out to the gathering, found a space on the floor, and sat down next to Buddy. He and I talked as the night went on. He was smoking a joint and offered one to me, but I was good with the wine. He was talking about the toll touring takes on a person. How you fly into a city, do a concert, fly out of the city to another, do a concert, fly out of that city to yet another city, do a concert, and repeat that till you have no sense of time or space. And then you eventually get home, and you just collapse. Then it starts all over again. He said this between drags on his joint.

"Jimi is flying to London tomorrow," he told me. "On Air India. The band's playing the Isle of Wight Festival."

I was thinking that I hoped the flight would not be early in the morning, because it was getting late, but then again, I don't think it would have affected Jimi, because he was such a night owl. Buddy then told me that after Jimi had left Electric Lady, he told Devon to get out of his life. But that was always happening.

About three in the morning, I went into the kitchen to say goodbye to Jimi, who was there talking to some girl. Surprisingly, Jimi wasn't wasted. He was in a good mood. Given what had happened earlier at the launch party, causing Jimi to storm out, I didn't want to say anything about Electric Lady. So I said that I'd heard from Buddy that he was going to England to play the Isle of Wright festival, and I asked if there was any progress on the legal stuff.

Jimi told me only that he would be seeing Chas Chandler when he was in London, and he wanted Chas' take on going in a new musical direction with more band members.

"Get ready, man. Get ready for the next trip," he told me. I could see he was really psyched about whatever he had in his mind. Then the conversation drifted off, and before it got awkward, I said goodnight and told him we should get together when he got back. Knowing that people come and go a lot in the Village, he gave me the key to the apartment should I ever need to make a pit stop. Not to stay, but to hang out now and then. It seemed a little odd, but I thanked him, took the key, and left.

It was the last time I saw Jimi alive.

The next time I heard from Jimi, it was also the last time, was on September 15 or 16, I don't remember exactly.

I received what I refer to as "the call." Jimi woke me up very early in the morning, calling from a London pay phone (a "coin box" over there). He sounded good. He was in good spirits and was simply checking in to tell me he was anxious to pick up where we'd left off once he got back to New York. I didn't know what to make of it as Jimi had never called me before; I would always call him. Thinking about it the next day, I didn't understand why he couldn't have called from his hotel or apartment. I figured I would ask him when he got back to NYC. Unfortunately, I never got the chance.

Jimi died less than four weeks after the Electric Lady launch party. He never returned to the recording studio in which he'd invested so much time and effort. In total, Jimi spent only ten weeks recording in Electric Lady, mostly during the final phases of construction. He made his last studio recording of a new solo demo called "Belly Button Window," on August 22. The last mix session with Eddie Kramer took place on August 24, for "Freedom," "Night Bird Flying," "Dolly Dagger," and "Belly Button Window."

John Storyk said it best: "Unlike most studios of that era, Electric Lady is really the dawn of a new studio. Now, every artist has their own studio. The idea that the artist was on that side of the glass was a relatively new idea. Most control rooms were small; they were for engineers. Artists were on the other side of the glass. They come in, they go out, 'Have a nice day.' This was completely different." The way I see it, Jimi was a visionary.

Postscript: In early 2000, Electric Lady fell into financial hardship and disarray before it was taken over and renovated by an investor named Keith Stoltz and his studio manager, Lee Foster. As a result, Electric Lady came roaring back. Several years ago, I had the opportunity to visit the studio with my two daughters, and I met Lee Foster. He graciously showed us around. It was the first time I had been there since the launch party. I barely remembered it. It seemed like Lee had added recording studios to the original Studio A and Studio B. Before I left, I told him that I had taken pictures of Jimi recording and that I would enlarge one, frame it, and bring it to him as a gift that he could hang on the wall in the studio that Jimi had built.

Electric Lady Studios has been made famous by sessions in the 1970s not just with Jimi Hendrix but with The Rolling Stones, Led Zeppelin, Stevie Wonder, David Bowie, John Lennon, and Patti Smith, among others. And it is once again a popular location for mainstream artists today, including U2, Taylor Swift, and Lady Gaga. Electric Lady still maintains its reputation as a hallowed ground for recorded music. It is the oldest working and thriving recording studio in New York City.

25

September 18, 1970

After Jimi went to London that final time, I often thought about using his apartment now that he had given me the keys, but at first, I couldn't bring myself to do it. I felt that I would be betraying a trust, or maybe I thought it would have been too much of a hanger-on thing to do, especially since I was so adamant about staying under the radar. I always tried to keep my relationship with Jimi professional even though it eventually became a friendship.

I had a date later that evening, and we agreed to meet at Kettle of Fish, the small Greenwich Village bar that was a musicians' hangout.

I'd ended up with a couple of hours to kill that evening, and since I was already in the Village, I nervously decided to take Jimi up on his offer to use his apartment. He was out of the country, so I figured, what the hell?

Fifty-Nine West Twelfth Street is a seventeen-story Art Deco building built in 1931. The doormen knew me from my many script-writing visits; that, plus I had answered many of the doormen's calls when unexpected "girlfriends" and groupies showed up—sometimes a parade.

It was the only apartment Jimi ever lived in while in New York; he called it his home.

The building was converted to condos in 1986. Next door to what had been Jimi's eleventh-floor apartment, Academy Award–winning actress Marisa Tomei eventually moved in, and the filmmaker John Waters lived a few floors below. Cameron Diaz bought a condo in the same building right below Jimi's in 2008 for $2.9 million. It was thought to be Jimi's apartment; it wasn't. She ended up selling the apartment in 2016 for $4.25 million. The apartment Jimi lived in was sold for $5.62 million in 2013 to Frederick Baer, which was more money than Jimi ever earned during his lifetime as a rock superstar. He was worth $800,000 when he died.

As I entered the apartment early that evening, the place seemed disconcertingly quiet. As I mentioned, it had a nice, flowing, loft-like layout. It was a prewar building, and the location was great. For me it was too quiet, so I turned on the TV. That day the apartment dully contrasted the times when music was blaring and I would walk in on a horny, adoring, or just plain curious bevy of hippie ladies. I glanced at the phone, expecting it to ring. Sometimes it never stopped ringing. So many people had Jimi's phone number that someone once suggested he put in two more lines. That still wouldn't have handled all the calls.

It was the first time I had come to the apartment without Jimi's being there, and it felt weird. There were three sofas low to the floor, and lots of throw pillows. Moroccan and

African bedspreads and prayer rugs covered the ceiling and walls. There were lots of rugs, as I mentioned earlier. One piece I really liked was a framed artwork with broken pieces of mirror set in clay, very avant-garde. Jimi had made it for the apartment himself. It reminded me of a late Picasso.

Previously when I'd been there, the apartment had been really cool, but now with the emptiness, the wall hangings made the room claustrophobic, giving it an eerie feel, almost otherworldly. Like being in a Moroccan tent after all the Moroccans had fled. And it was dark, except for the one lamp I turned on.

Okay, I said to myself, *enough of this*. I went to the kitchen, found a half a bottle of white wine in the fridge, and poured myself a glass. It was probably left over from Jimi's Electric Lady opening afterparty three weeks before, on the night before he left for London. I went back into the living room and sat on the ridiculously low sofa.

Starting to feel it wasn't fun being alone in the apartment, I got up and went to the front window. Jimi's apartment was across the street from the New School, a private research university, which was founded by a small group of prominent intellectuals and educators. At the time, the famous anthropologist and author Margaret Meade was teaching classes in anthropology there. I stood at the window looking down at the pretend hippie students below, mulling around the narrow and tall glass-walled entrance to the college, and at the "professional" hippies hanging out up and down the block—there were usually a couple of them strumming guitars while sitting on a stoop. I got a kick out of thinking, *If they only knew who lived across the street.*

Then it happened.

September 18, 1970

I heard a newscaster's voice from the TV: "Rock guitarist Jimi Hendrix was found dead today in a London apartment." There was something about a drug overdose.

I must have leapt across the room, because the next thing I knew I was standing in front of the TV looking at footage of Jimi in his white fringe leather shirt onstage at Woodstock.

Totally surreal. Here I was in Jimi Hendrix's apartment, drinking his wine, looking at his television set while hearing the news that he was dead.

I felt surprise, disbelief, irony. It couldn't have happened. It wasn't right. Jimi had always been more into music than drugs.

I had to get out of his place. My being there suddenly felt all wrong. I quickly left.

The first few days after Jimi's death are still hazy to me. I know I slept a lot. I didn't know how to deal with the news. I was shocked and sad. I had grown very fond of Jimi, and collaborating with him had become a very special part of my life. I'd hoped that the project had meant something to him and that he wanted it to succeed.

A week after his death, I gathered the many photographs that I had shot at Woodstock and in the various recording studios around town, in the form of slides. Unfortunately, none were from Electric Lady. Bob Levine called, and I told him I had about three or four dozen slides of Jimi no one had seen. Bob invited me to come to his and Kathy's apartment on West Fifty-Seventh Street the following night with the slides and a slide projector.

When I got there, Bob opened a bottle of wine. For the next hour, I projected those slides up on a bare wall, and we just sat and reflected on Jimi. We shared stories, we shed tears, we laughed a little bit, and we just immersed ourselves in all of our memories of him. We mourned.

Then it was time to go. I packed up my slide projector, said goodbye to both, and left. It was the last time I would see either of them. Spending that time with Bob and Kathy, watching how they looked at each other and interacted, I knew that they were very much in love. It was so obvious. Maybe it had been that way all along, and I'd never noticed, or hadn't wanted to notice.

When I walked out of the building that night, I could feel a chapter of my life closing behind me. I wasn't sure what would come next. I didn't have the energy to analyze it too much at that moment. I just figured, as it had always happened with me, that something would come along. Some new thing would just carry me away.

Bob and Kathy eventually married, moved to Florida, and stayed together for the rest of their lives. No matter how unconventional their relationship was, it stood the test of time. They were an inspirational love story.

26

The Death of Jimi Hendrix

Providing details about Jimi's death is almost impossible. It should have been a simple open-and-closed case. But there are so many unsubstantiated "facts"—statements made that were only to be denied, altered, or contradicted completely later; rumors; bizarre conspiracy theories; pre-meditated lies; half-truths; overlooked or wrongly interpreted facts—that what really happened can no longer be separated from all the fiction to determine what actually happened. What I know is that the official cause of Jimi's death was listed as asphyxiation due to a barbiturate overdose. It's believed that Jimi had taken a combination of pills and alcohol, but the alcohol was never verified. It was supposedly red wine. He was found unconscious in a London hotel room by his local hookup, Monika Dannemann, who claimed she had been sleeping in the room with him. She called for an ambulance, but Jimi was pronounced dead on arrival at St. Mary Abbots Hospital. There's so much ongoing speculation, controversy, and inconsistency in the accounts surrounding Jimi's death, even to this day, that we may never know the truth. There was even a story, which some believe, that Jimi was murdered, arranged by Michael Jeffery.

Maybe the best way to understand what happened is to go back to the days that led up to Jimi's death.

Jimi left New York the day after I last saw him at his West Twelfth Street apartment and arrived in London on August 27, where he conducted a series of interviews. From there he went to the Isle of Wight, which turned out to be the largest single audience of his career. It didn't help that he had technical problems with his amps. They were picking up radio signals. Jimi had a cold and was totally exhausted. On top of that, he had to go on at two a.m. If that wasn't bad enough, less than twenty-four hours later, they were playing a gig at an amusement park in Stockholm, Sweden, where, I was told, Jimi insulted the audience, who was constantly calling out for his hits. The next day, the band, still being billed as The Jimi Hendrix Experience, traveled to Gothenburg for an outdoor gig.

The Isle of Wight Festival appearance kicked off a week of intensive touring. At the Isle of Wight, people noticed Jimi and Miles Davis were hanging out and talking about working together; Jimi was telling whoever would listen to him that he wanted to be taken seriously as a musician and that he didn't want to play the guitar with his teeth anymore.

Over the next seven days, Jimi, Billy Cox, and Mitch Mitchell would play six major gigs in three countries across Europe, and Michael Jeffery would have them do more, but the tour was cut short after concerns for the health of Billy Cox. Somewhere, sometime on September 1, someone spiked Billy's drink with LSD, and he was still paranoid and exhausted more than a week later. On September 9, the tour was canceled, and Billy Cox returned to the U.S. Even though none of them realized it at the time, they played their last gig together at the Open Air Love & Peace Festival in Fehmarn, Germany, on September 6.

The "Love & Peace Festival" on the isle of Fehmarn, which is located off the coast of northern Germany in the Baltic Sea, was intended to be the European answer to Woodstock. Instead, it turned into something more like Altamont. Like Woodstock it was drenched by storms, but unlike Woodstock it was overrun by a German biker gang, and it was plagued by cancellations from big-name acts. By the time Jimi got there, it was chaotic, filled with violence and arson. This is what Jimi faced for his last live performance. Interesting to note that Jimi didn't want to come to Europe in the first place, but Jeffery convinced Jimi the new Electric Lady Studios needed an infusion of cash, so Jeffery booked Jimi on a short tour that began at the Isle of Wight, continued in Denmark and Sweden, and ended in Germany.

Chas Chandler was in the audience. He was seeing Jimi for the first time since having parted ways a year before. Chas wasn't impressed. In an interview he gave, Chas said Jimi was a wreck, that he would start a song and then wouldn't even remember what song they were playing. Chas remarked, "It was really awful to watch." At the after party is when Billy Cox's drink was spiked. This had a terrible effect on Billy because he was truly drug-free. He never did drugs, and because he didn't, Billy was a stabilizing influence on Jimi, but this surprise assault caused Billy to experience a nightmarish bad trip that, combined with the stress of a busy schedule, over the next few days put him dangerously close to a nervous breakdown. It didn't help that Jimi had a feverish cold the night he played in Arhus, Denmark, and had to cut short his set after only three numbers.

On September 3, Mitch got a phone call telling him that his wife had given birth to a baby girl. That's all he needed to hear; Mitchell chartered a flight back to London, and he took Billy Cox with him, but first they met up with Jimi later that day in Copenhagen for a gig. Jimi was over the worst of his cold, and when he came on stage, he was invigorated. The reviews of the show were glowing. One reviewer remarked, "As a warrior of love, he stood dressed in many colours and was the best guitarist rock 'n' roll music can offer.'

The band regrouped and flew on to Berlin to perform at the Super Concert '70, an indoor festival at the city's Deutschland-halle. He followed that with a series of sit-down interviews, then took off to Berlin, from where he flew to Hamburg, after that to Grossenbrode, and finally arrived on the isle of Fehmarn on Saturday afternoon. The promoters had timed the event to coincide with the Isle of Wight Festival, with the aim of snagging some major acts, including Jimi who was at the height of his popularity in Germany because of the Wood-stock movie. Unfortunately, biker gangs, overcrowding, bad weather, and numerous cancellations had soured the "Love & Peace" attitude of the crowd.

The band arrived on the site by eleven a.m., having been rescheduled for midday. An increasingly paranoid Billy Cox was on the verge of having a nervous breakdown—according to the band's roadies, they noticed he was very paranoid about what was going on. Billy was fearful that the stage was going to collapse, and everybody was going to be killed. They convinced him to make it through the show, that it was the last show, to get it over with and then he could get out of there. According to the promoters and stagehands who were there, Jimi was very friendly. They found him to be a gentle, nice guy, very laid back.

When the band took the stage at around one o'clock in the afternoon, they were greeted with boos and jeers and shouts of "Hau ab!" (German for "go home" or "get lost"). Jimi didn't let it bother him. He even was comical by joining in with the booing. He then confronted the crowd saying, "I don't give a fuck if you boo," he shrugs, "as long as you boo in tune, you mothers...." That caused the booing to stop and he tore into Howlin' Wolf's "Killing Floor." Unbeknownst to everyone, "Killing Floor" was the opening song of the first-ever Jimi Hendrix Experience's gig in October 1966 in Paris. When he finished the song, the crowd exploded in an ocean of cheers. He won them over.

It's been documented that the last two songs Hendrix ever played live were "Purple Haze" and a stormy version of "Voodoo Child (Slight Return)" ending the song with the final lines he would ever sing in public, "If I don't see you no more in this world/I'll meet you in the next one and don't be late, don't be late.'

You can read into this anything you want, but just a few days before, Jimi was interviewed by *Melody Maker*, and he was optimistic. A brief excerpt from that article says it all. Jimi said, "Something new has got to come, and Jimi Hendrix will be there. I want a big band. I don't mean three harps and fourteen violins; I mean a big band full of competent musicians that I can conduct and write for. And with the music we will paint pictures of Earth and space, so that the listener can be taken somewhere.... They are getting their minds ready now.

Like me, they are going back home, getting fat and making themselves ready for the next trip."

Jimi returned to London, the place he considered home, where he once told me he felt the most comfortable. Once there he hooked up with Monika Dannemann. Monika was a twenty-five-year-old German ex-figure skater, who, it turned out, was obsessed with Jimi. What Jimi didn't know was that Monika got to London in August and was just waiting for Jimi to get back from his European tour. She planned to ambush him into being with her. Monika originally got together with Jimi through Alvenia Bridges, a Black woman from Kansas who, years later, became the tour manager for The Rolling Stones. If Alvenia hadn't stepped in, then Monika would probably never have met Jimi. From all accounts, Monika was delusional. She created a fantasy relationship in her mind with Jimi. I think I can safely say that she was just another one of Jimi's flings, nothing more. Yet, after only a few days, Monika told anyone who would listen that she and Jimi were soulmates and had gotten engaged. After Jimi's death, a seemingly bereaved Monika told the press that Jimi had fallen madly in love with her and they were planning on getting married, but she left out one small detail—Jimi already had a fiancée at the time, Danish model and actress Kirsten Nefer.

Monika was an obsessive fan who had the capacity to harm Jimi, the object of her sick adoration. Monika made a lot more out of the relationship than it was. Not one person even remotely close to Jimi ever said that he had any intention of marrying her. They accused her of having invented everything. She was also verbally abusive to Jimi, and even Jimi said he thought she could be violent. Yet she tried to invent an image of Jimi and her being so happy and in love. The fact is, Jimi only knew her for a few days. Several of Jimi's friends thought Monika "was nuts." Mitch Mitchell more than once said that Monika was not the great love of Jimi's life, and that Monika exaggerated her affair with Jimi. Eric Burdon went so far as to say Monika was not only genuinely crazy, but was a stalker as well. Ginger Baker claimed she wasn't mentally stable.

Unfortunately, when Jimi returned to London from touring, against the advice of close friends, he called up Monika, probably because she was one of his easily available flings. Monika had already rented a room at the Samarkand Hotel in Notting Hill in anticipation. Before retiring to the room, Jimi dropped in at a popular London club that was a magnet for rockers, Ronny Scott's, to see Eric Burdon's new group, War. In the club was Paul Almond, a young, charismatic entertainment attorney from America who represented War. Paul was introduced to Jimi, and Jimi joined Paul at his table as they waited for Burdon. The two of them spent some time talking about the music business. He found Jimi surprisingly friendly, soft spoken, almost shy, open, bright, and completely aware and mentally agile. He was in a positive frame of mind. While at Ronny Scott's, Jimi jammed with Eric Burdon, playing guitar on a couple of songs, but he didn't sing or play any of his own numbers. As was the case with Jimi when he was in a club in New York, he would just get up and play. He loved to just play. I think he enjoyed playing these impromptu gigs in clubs more than huge concert halls because he didn't have to "perform." It was small, quiet, intimate, and just about the music. Eventually, he wound up back at Monika's. She claimed that she made them both dinner at around eleven p.m., and then she drove Jimi to a small party at the London flat of music entrepreneur Pete Kameron. The interesting thing is that Monika was not invited to the party, nor did Jimi make any effort to take her in to the party to introduce her to as his fiancée, most likely because she wasn't his fiancée, and probably because Devon Wilson was going to be there. Monika was jealous with rage, and people witnessed her verbally accosting Jimi outside of the flat when he showed interest in another girl. At the gathering was Angie Burdon; Stella Douglas, Alan Douglas' wife and one of Jimi's traveling companions to Morocco; financier Burt Kleiner; Wimpy fast food chain owner, David Salmon; and Devon Wilson, who had flown over from New York. To Devon, Jimi seemed agitated when he arrived, probably because of his argument with Monika in front of the building.

After causing a scene outside, she repeatedly pressed the apartment intercom. Guests repeatedly told her to go away. Jimi never bothered to answer, so she left. However, Jimi did ask her to come back and pick him up, and she did. She came back at nearly three a.m. and caused a scene yet again. She was angry after learning that Jimi had spoken with Kathy Etchingham earlier in the afternoon.

Jimi left with Monika and returned to Samarkand. This is where things got murky. All these years later, the hours between the time they entered her room at the Samarkand and the time the ambulance drivers entered the same room to find Jimi's body covered in his own vomit, remain a complete mystery. Stories and accounts have repeatedly changed over time, and the truth of what really happened that night may never be known. What allegedly happened, and most of the reports came from Monika so their accuracy is dubious, is that Monika picked Jimi up from the party and, according to her, asked Jimi if he wanted to pass by a local London bar, the speakeasy to see Mitch before they went back to Samarkand.

Jimi supposedly said that Mitch could wait, that he wanted to go back to the flat and spend the time with Monika. Monika claimed that Mitch wanted to see Jimi and jam, but Jimi didn't want to. The most likely reason as to why Jimi wasn't interested in going into the speakeasy for a jam was because he didn't have his guitar. It was in the Samarkand basement flat. It should also be noted that Jimi and Mitch were hardly communicating after Jimi became annoyed with Mitch when Karen Davis and Mitch became an "item" in early September during the European tour.

Monika and Jimi arrived back at the Samarkand basement flat at around three a.m. There was only one witness the night Jimi died, and that was Monika Dannemann, who kept changing her story so she couldn't be held accountable for Jimi's death. The rest of the so-called authors are only speculating as to what happened, and they have no idea since they weren't there, including me, and many used secondhand quotes to explain what happened from people who have contradicted themselves. Monika originally told police that after picking Jimi up from the party, the two spent the entire night talking (in other statements she gave, she said arguing), until 7:15 a.m. Monika said she was exhausted and needed to take a pill and go to sleep. Jimi reportedly asked Monika if she had any sleeping pills he could take to sleep. She offered him a strong German pill called Vesparax.

Vesparax wasn't normally prescribed by doctors as a sleeping pill. It was a barbiturate, and it was heavy stuff. The drug was prescribed for people that had personality disorders to control mood swings and to keep them under control. It was used for treating schizophrenia or bipolar disorder. Vesparax has been discontinued in most countries around the world.

It started declining in use during the early '80s because of the danger it posed to people who used it, and other new drugs were developed that took its place. It was a powerful three-combination drug tablet that also helped the person sleep, but it wasn't a strong "sleeping pill"—far from it. Monika referred to it as a "sleeping tablet." The instructions and warnings that came with the drug were in German, and Jimi wouldn't have been able to read them. It's very likely that Monika didn't tell Jimi the potency of the pills, that he had no idea how potent they were. In all, Jimi took nine tablets.

Monika claimed she was prescribed these pills because of an ice-skating injury, but it's most likely a doctor would have prescribed a different medication for the injury she had suffered. Vesparax had sedative and hypnotic properties, with a short-acting barbiturate and a long-acting barbiturate. The short-acting Secobarbital performed as a sedative, and the side effects caused confusion, nausea, vomiting, and difficulty breathing. Those were all the symptoms Jimi was most likely experiencing, and the high dose of nine pills exacerbated the effects. There are people, mostly the press, that believe Jimi was a junkie and addicted to hard drugs. He wasn't.

Monika's timeline of events has changed at least a dozen times, and it is riddled with inconsistencies, but in Monika's most generally accepted story, she said that she found Jimi and that she went out for a pack of cigarettes. When she came back, she noticed he had thrown up and couldn't wake up. She claims to have immediately called Alvenia Bridges, who had spent the night with Eric Burdon, and told Alvenia that Jimi had taken some sleeping pills and was sick, and that she couldn't wake him. Burdon got on the phone and instructed Monika to turn Jimi over and spent several minutes trying to convince her to call an ambulance. She was apparently scared that she would get in trouble. Burdon verbally forced her to call an ambulance. While waiting for the ambulance to arrive, she hid Jimi's guitar thinking the case might have had some cannabis in it. She finally called an ambulance at 11:18 a.m., and it arrived just nine minutes later. Burdon got out of bed and made his way to the scene, but his accounts have also changed over the years. In some stories, he arrived while Jimi was still lying on the bed, and in others, Jimi was already in the ambulance. Yet, according to the two paramedics, when they got there, the door was open, and they just walked right in. There was no one immediately around, but Jimi's body was on the bed. They had to radio for the police from the van, and they couldn't touch anything in the flat. They reported that they knew he was gone, that he was on top of the bed, dressed, but they didn't recognize him. He was in a pool of his own vomit. It was everywhere. They reported that the vomit was all dried and Jimi had been lying there for a long time. There was no heartbeat.

The version of events presented by Monika Dannemann was accepted as fact, in spite of inconsistencies, backtracking, and contradictory statements, for twenty years. Over the years, her statements and explanations about Jimi's death have been universally discredited. She was a German figure-skater who suffered an injury, quit figure skating, became a drug-taker, was delusional, and had fantasized to the point that she believed her own lies, but she was the one who was with Jimi the night he died. Claims she made about that night were denied in almost every detail by all the authorities involved.

It is assumed that Monika panicked that morning and instead of calling for the ambulance, called Alvenia and Eric

Burdon first for help. Either this delay contributed to Jimi's death, or he had already been dead for a while. According to Monika, the flat at the Samarkand hotel was a "home" to Jimi, but Jimi was not living there, and Jimi had only a few belongings there; most of his possessions were actually at the Cumberland hotel. In all probability, Jimi returned to Samarkand with Monika only to retrieve his guitar. It was not the cozy love nest Monika wanted everyone to believe. It is known that she argued violently with Jimi before he died, and it was her barbiturates that Jimi had in his system. After Jimi's death, her story changed every time she told it. She even claimed that she had poems and love letters that Jimi wrote to her, but she refused to show them to anyone because they were "too personal." What is probably more likely is that hey probably didn't exist and that she made them up so as not to appear to be just another one of Jimi's sexed out groupies, nothing more to Jimi than another fling.

Then the conspiracy theories started to take hold, the most prominent, or the most absurd, depending on your outlook, being that Jimi was murdered by Mike Jeffery. This claim was made by one of Jimi's roadies, who wrote a book in which he made the claim that Jeffery had Jimi killed because Jimi was going to leave him. In the same book, he said there was a government conspiracy, but he was confused as to which government wanted Jimi killed, the U.S or the U.K. Then, of course, there's Monika, who, in one of her many changing stories, said in 1975 on a radio interview that she had "proof" that the Mafia murdered Jimi.

It's no secret that her whole life, Monika was always looking to escape blame for Jimi's death. You've got to question the mental stability, or instability to be more accurate, of a person like that—one who would create an entire fantasy relationship around what was only a few days spent with Jimi. After Jimi died, she went back to Germany where she was photographed a week later smiling and happy in her apartment, not grieving for her deceased "fiancé." After that, Monika was only interested in discussing her new career as a painter of Jimi Hendrix portraits. Sharon Lawrence, a reporter friend of Jimi's, said Monika's strange detachment was creepy. But then again, Sharon Lawrence herself started the claim that Jimi took his own life, that he committed suicide. She said he killed himself because everyone wanted something from him; he was overworked; he was exhausted; he was in a bad state physically and emotionally; and he hated being famous. All of that pushed him over the edge.

The press reports written immediately after Jimi died suggested that Jimi died as a result of a massive drug overdose. The more sensationalist papers called him a drug addict, and another said illicit drugs were responsible for his death. After the inquest, however, all the insinuations disappeared and were replaced by the real cause of Jimi's death—inhalation of vomit due to barbiturate intoxication.

The people who were closest to Jimi, like Kathy and, especially, Bob Levine, had nothing but good things to say. Bob Levine believed and even said that "Jimi Hendrix died by accident. He was a happy guy, looking forward to making music. And Michael Jeffery didn't have it out for Jimi in any way. I talked to him the day before Jimi died. He had major plans for Jimi." Michael Jeffery even said some very flattering things about Jimi after he died, especially about Jimi's growing spirituality and true persona; he remarked that Jimi was a quiet, introspective, highly intelligent, and very talented man. Jeffery was so upset by Jimi's death that he couldn't leave his car at Jimi's funeral. Chas Chandler said that the stories coming out in the press about Jimi being a gloomy, sad person were totally untrue; Jimi was just the opposite; he was full of life and fun. Chas said that Jimi's death was the tragedy, unlike his real life. There were others as well, journalists who interviewed him right before his death, and even Paul Almond who had the last in-depth discussion with Jimi, that all said that Jimi was in a positive frame of mind and that he was planning for the future. I couldn't agree more, because that's the Jimi Hendrix I experienced, an artist looking toward the future, full of creative juices and optimism. He had booked his ticket to New York, and he was looking forward to getting back to Electric Lady.

In spite of what the conspiracy theories are trying to prove, the simple fact is that Jimi took more pills than the prescribed amount, and the overdose put him in a comatose state that affected his breathing. It was probably a simple case of confusion that spun into tragedy. He was on his back when he became sick and was unable to turn over when he started vomiting. Jimi's other girlfriends stated that Jimi sometimes choked in his sleep and had sleep apnea, so the combination of the potency of those pills with his sleeping disorder meant he didn't stand a chance.

It's all documented on Jimi's death certificate. There was dry vomit completely blocking his airways, which confirmed the inhalation and suffocation. The autopsy results state very clearly inhalation of vomit due to barbiturate intoxication. The doctor who conducted the autopsy said there were no signs that Jimi deliberately intended to commit suicide, so he ruled it an accidental barbiturate overdose.

The funeral was held in Seattle. Miles Davis was a pallbearer. Devon Wilson went with Miles to the funeral. Mitch and Noel were both there. Everyone close to Jimi was there. Johnny Winter performed. Kathy Etchingham, who was probably the love of Jimi's life, did not go. A monument was later erected at Renton Cemetery in honor of Jimi that was commissioned by his sister, Janie Hendrix, so that fans could pay their respects. It replaced the simple one that was placed there decades earlier.

As time went on, Monika didn't stop with her fabrications and outrageous stories. She made her living painting and selling Jimi Hendrix portraits and lived her life all about Jimi Hendrix and the fantasy she created about the two of them. After Jimi's death, every interview Monika gave continually changed about what happened that morning, and she continued the fabrication, which, by now, she probably believed to be true, that she and Jimi were going to be married. However, all this time, Monika was attacking and accusing Kathy of being a liar. Eventually, Kathy had enough, and she was forced to go to court when Monika continued to repeat the libel that Kathy was an "inveterate liar" about her life with Jimi, and that she had stolen belongings from Jimi's London flat. Kathy felt compelled to set the record straight, not so much for herself, but for the sake of her children. Kathy Etchingham decided that she had to once and for all learn the real truth about Jimi's death.

In the early '90s, Kathy commissioned her own investigation into Jimi's death. She spent three years investigating, trying to find out what Monika's pills were doing in Jimi's body and how they got there. She eventually said, "We never really got to the bottom of what her (Dannemann's) tablets were doing in him. I doubt we ever will." Kathy also wanted an investigation into the inconsistencies in Monika's story. Monika kept changing the time she woke up and noticed when Jimi was in trouble. There was a delay in calling the ambulance, so it was assumed that this delay may have contributed to Jimi's death. Instead of ringing for the ambulance when Monika realized Jimi was in trouble, she called Eric Burdon who forced her to call an ambulance. She never revealed the strength of the pills to Jimi and also led him to believe they were sleeping pills. Perhaps, if Jimi had known the strength of the pills he was taking, he might not have taken them. It was Monika's responsibility to tell Jimi since she was familiar with the safe dosage of the drug. Kathy felt Monika had no excuse for not revealing the potency of the drug.

Kathy's investigation was thorough. She learned all the facts through the hospital medical documents, autopsy reports, and business contracts. Kathy dismisses all the "Jimi was murdered" and suicide claims. Everything showed that Jimi died from barbiturate poisoning caused by an overdose. Kathy exposed Monika's lies. It came out that the fantasy stories Monika created about her life with Jimi were designed to make it look like she was in no way responsible for Jimi's death. It went to court, and it all came out during the investigation and court case.

Monika spent two decades lying about her relationship with Jimi and the circumstances of his death, and it was all exposed. She lived only for Jimi, even after he died. She even had photos doctored. There's a picture of Jimi and Monika surrounded by a whole group of other people that was taken in Germany; Monika had all the other people in the picture removed so as to make it look like she and Jimi were having a romantic night out, just the two of them. Monika went out and did whatever she had to in order to keep the myth of her relationship with Jimi alive.

During Kathy's investigation, Monika hired a private detective to prove that what she said about the events the morning Jimi died were true. It was speculated that Monika needed to have her stories verified because everything she said back then was being scrutinized by Kathy's investigation. Monika probably panicked and needed to protect herself from being held responsible. I suppose Monika knew everything she was lying about would come out through Etchingham's investigation.

When Jimi died, people pretty much just took her word as to what happened and never questioned her on her contradictions. The court case was ready to confront her on her lies and her fabricated stories. She was now facing the scrutiny over Jimi's death that she should have faced back in 1970, not decades later. Monika came from a conservative family and most likely didn't want to be seen as just another sex-crazed groupie who was in reality stalking Jimi.

With Monika's suicide in 1996, she took the truth of Jimi's final hours to her grave. To this day, Jimi's passing remains a mystery that's still clouded by hearsay, rumors, and lies that have become part of rock 'n' roll folklore. But more importantly, as the controversy surrounding his death fades, what remains is Jimi's essence; Jimi's flamboyance; Jimi's passion; Jimi's style; Jimi's virtuosity, and his inspiration. He's as relevant today as he was more than fifty years ago. He continues to inspire music to this day.

Jimi and Me

I think Kathy Etchingham said it best when she said that she wants Jimi to be remembered as not only a guitar superstar but as a truly lovely person. He was. I will always remember him as being a kind, giving, gentle, fun person with a great sense of humor, who just so happened to be a musical genius.

27

After Jimi

In the first year after Jimi's death, I traveled a bit. I went to London. I went back to California, and I kept writing— all kinds of ideas, stories, scripts; whatever came to mind. And I continued with my photography, but eventually that leveled off.

Regarding the script for *Avril*, a girl I was dating in Woodstock presented it to Todd Rundgren to see if he might be interested in being involved with the music. Todd read it and felt it was too violent. I reread it myself at that point and agreed. So I connected with a friend from college, Joe Schulman, and we carved out some of the violence and actually made it a better script. Still no dialogue. But nothing ever happened with Todd. As I recall, Nancy Wilson from the band Heart also had some marginal interest in developing the script, but nothing ever came of that either. I ended up putting it in a folder and filing it away.

As time went on, my career took shape. Over the years, as a writer and a producer, I have been involved in hundreds of interesting projects. I've been president of production for Greenwich Studios in Florida, where *Miami Vice*, *Ace Ventura Pet Detective*, *True Lies*, and many other films and TV series were produced. I've been CEO of the Television Theater Company in New York. I became a member of the National Academy of Television Arts and Sciences, the Writers Guild of America (WGA), the Producers Guild of America (PGA), and many other industry organizations. I've won several industry awards for TV series and movies I produced. I've produced or executive-produced and written several TV series, specials, and movies.

But through all that I've done in my career, the time that I still think burns brightest is the time I spent with Jimi Hendrix. Being that close to a shooting star was a transcendent experience.

About twenty years ago, Jimi's estate approached me to ask about purchasing many of the photos that I had taken of him. I met with the lawyer representing the estate, and we made a deal for the pictures. In hindsight, I wish I had licensed them as opposed to selling them outright. But I didn't know that much twenty years ago. All I requested was that my name always appear as a photo credit, and the estate has been very diligent about that.

On October 22, 2012, Hurricane Sandy devastated the Jersey Coast, where I was living. My eleven-year-old daughter, Audrey, and I were forced to vacate our beach home due to the storm's approach. Just before we left, I moved everything valuable and needed by my family to the attic, just in case the house would be flooded. And indeed, our home was damaged and flooded when we returned a few days later.

Arriving home, my daughter and I immediately went to the attic to assess the items we had hoped would be spared from damage. While we were going through the boxes and items, my daughter began poking around the dark corners of the attic and came upon an envelope lying on top of a pile of old papers I had not touched in decades. Not sure what she had found, Audrey ran over to me with it.

To my shock and surprise, the envelope contained nineteen rare, unpublished negatives still in their original protective plastic sheets. They were pictures I had taken on August 18, 1969, of Jimi Hendrix during his performance at Woodstock, and many more of him and Gypsy Sun and Rainbows as he was forming the band and recording at The Hit Factory in NYC.

The second my daughter placed them in my hands, everything about Jimi flashed before my eyes...from the day I met Jimi to the day I cried when I heard he'd been found dead.

Pulling her down to sit next to me, I said, "These are photos of the greatest guitar player that ever lived, and he was my friend, and his name is Jimi Hendrix." The storm took a lot of things from me, and many people, but it also gave me fond memories of a great time, and of a great man. A man who, for reasons still unknown to me until this day, had chosen me and given me access to his life to take photos, and had referred to me as a friend.

After spending hours sharing stories of me and Jimi with my daughter, I safely stored the negatives away. I pulled them out from time to time over the years to relive those moments or to share stories with friends and relatives at dinner parties.

Then one day I finally reached out to John McDermott, who co-runs and manages the Jimi Hendrix estate, Experience Hendrix, with Jimi's sister. He knew Janie would be interested in them, so he arranged a meeting. Janie was coming to New York, and evidently, whenever she visited, she took over an office at Electric Lady Studios. Perfectly appropriate. And so that's where the meeting was to take place. When I met her that afternoon, I was quite impressed. She was very smart and obviously was doing a great job in helping to grow the legacy of her late brother. I think she deserves a great deal of credit for Jimi's legacy.

I showed her and John the slides in their plastic binders. Janie really liked the pictures, and they both told me they wanted to buy them. I said that I would license them, because I didn't want to make the same mistake of selling them outright. John said that they were interested only in purchasing them outright, and we did not make a deal that day.

Then Janie said to me, "Would you like some lunch?" And she fixed up a batch of delicious linguine with clam sauce in the kitchen at the studio. I think the reason she and I connected even though we didn't make a deal was the fact that I'd known her brother. I'd had a firsthand connection with him.

The three of us met again a year or two later to discuss a merchandising project, and she could not have been any more charming. The deal never happened, but it wasn't because of her or John; they wanted it to happen. Again, I thoroughly respect and appreciate how she works on her brother's behalf. John McDermott deserves much credit, too.

On a side note, in the early 1970s, I sold three images of Jimi to a company that was going to create a series of posters. The person buying them from me sent a bike messenger over to my apartment in New York, I was given a check for about $5,000, and I gave the messenger the three images. The next day the purchaser called me, furious, demanding to know where the pictures were. He had never received them. The bike messenger had made off with them, and they were never to be seen again. Or at least that's what I thought.

Around this time, I learned that Devon Wilson died on February 2, 1971. She either fell or jumped from an eight-floor window of the Chelsea Hotel. The true circumstances of her death are not known.

Two years later, in 1973, during an air traffic controller strike, I read somewhere that Michael Jeffery died along with sixty-three other people in a midair plane collision over Nantes, France. He was on his way to a meeting to determine the control of the Jimi Hendrix estate.

After that I went on with my life and rarely thought about any of those people and what I experienced until over forty-five years later when I was visiting American University in Washington, DC with my daughter Audrey who applied to college there.

While in Washington, we went to the Smithsonian. My other daughter Kathryn was on that trip as well, and the two of them wandered off to explore one wing while I went in another direction.

Soon after, they excitedly found me and pulled me over to the exhibit they had been looking at. It was a gallery full of famous rock 'n' roll stars. When I got over there, I could not believe what I saw. In one case were the three photos that had been stolen decades earlier. I'll never know exactly how they got there, but I can say with certainty that my work has been displayed at the Smithsonian Institute.

Avril lies in a desk drawer somewhere. Sometimes when I think about the story, I hear in my mind Jimi's guitar playing the sound of a lone rider coming into town and Paul

Butterfield's harmonica creating the eerie sound of pebbles falling on a coffin.

The dream of Electric Lady lives on. Here are just some who have recorded there: John Lennon, AC/DC, Led Zeppelin, Carly Simon, The Clash, Peter Frampton, The Rolling Stones, David Bowie, Al Green, Frank Zappa, Kanye West, Madonna, Bob Dylan, The Mighty Boosh, Courtney Love, Radiohead, Coldplay, Alice Cooper, Bad Religion, Stevie Wonder, Cactus, Goldfrapp, Greezy Wheels, Billy Cobham, Curtis Mayfield, Moby, the Mahavishnu Orchestra, Lou Reed, Mandrill, Muse, Arctic Monkeys, The Early Years, Sinéad O'Connor, Billy Joel, Billy Idol, Nas, The Mars Volta, Mike Oldfield, The Magnetic Fields, Guns N' Roses, Elkie Brooks, Patti Smith, John McLaughlin, KISS, Van Halen, Interpol, Ryan Adams, Steve Earle, Monster Magnet, The Pink Spiders, Deee-Lite, Chris Braide, Rancid, and Taylor Swift.

Famed Hendrix Shows

Jimi Hendrix is widely regarded as one of the most iconic musicians of all time. His career spanned only a few short years, but he left a lasting impact on the music industry. His virtuosic guitar playing, electrifying live performances, and groundbreaking approach to music cemented his place in history as a pioneer of the psychedelic and rock genres. Over the course of his career, he performed at countless concerts, but several stand out as the most famous and influential.

Fillmore West
February and June 1968

Jimi Hendrix's performances at the Fillmore West in San Francisco are legendary among his fans and music historians alike. Fillmore West was a popular music venue in the late 1960s, known for hosting some of the biggest and most influential names in rock music. Hendrix's shows at the venue are considered some of his finest live performances.

At the Fillmore West, Hendrix and his band played a mix of classic tracks, such as "Purple Haze" and "Hey Joe," as well as newer material, such as "Voodoo Child" and "I Don't Live Today." His guitar playing was electrifying, featuring intricate solos and an innovative use of effects pedals. Hendrix also demonstrated his versatility as a musician, playing both guitar and bass during the shows.

The Fillmore West shows are notable for their high energy and improvisational spirit. Hendrix and his band stretched out on their songs, often jamming for extended periods of time and exploring new musical ideas.

Atlanta International Pop Festival
July 3–5, 1970

Jimi Hendrix's show at the Atlanta International Pop Festival is widely regarded as one of his most impressive and powerful. The festival took place on July Fourth weekend in 1970 at the Middle Georgia Raceway in Byron, Georgia, and featured an impressive lineup of artists, including B. B. King, Johnny Winter, and Ten Years After.

Hendrix's set at the festival was a tour de force of guitar virtuosity and showmanship. He played a mix of classic tracks, such as "Purple Haze" and "Foxy Lady," as well as newer material, such as "Freedom" and "Message to Love." His guitar playing was explosive, once again featuring intricate solos and jaw-dropping displays of technical skill.

One of the most memorable moments of Hendrix's performance at the Atlanta festival was his cover of "The Star-Spangled Banner," which he had originally played at Woodstock. Hendrix's interpretation of the National Anthem was a powerful statement on the state of American society at the time, and his use of feedback and distortion to create the sounds of bombs and gunfire created an unforgettable sonic landscape.

The festival remains an important moment in the history of rock music, and Hendrix's performance is rightly regarded as one of its defining moments.

Los Angeles Forum
April 26, 1969

Jimi Hendrix's concert at the Forum in Inglewood, California, in 1969 is considered iconic. He and his band performed a blistering set of classic songs and new material. The performance was notable for its raw energy and improvisational spirit. He played classic tracks, such as "Hey Joe" and "Purple Haze," and new songs, such as "Room Full of Mirrors" and "I Don't Live Today." As with the other concerts, his guitar playing was electrifying.

One of the highlights of the show was Hendrix's performance of "Voodoo Child." He pushed his guitar playing to new heights, creating a wall of sound that left the audience in awe. The concert remains a touchstone for his fans.

Miami Pop Festival
December 28–30, 1968

The Miami Pop Festival in 1968 is regarded as one of Hendrix's most energetic and powerful shows. The festival took place at Gulfstream Park in Hallandale, Florida, and attracted over a hundred thousand people. Hendrix's set is notable for its raw energy and intensity. As with his other concerts, he played classic and new songs.

Isle of Wight Festival
August 26–30, 1970

Hendrix's performance at the Isle of Wight Festival in 1970 is considered one of his most memorable. The festival was held on the Isle of Wight, a small island off the coast of southern England, and attracted over six hundred thousand people.

Hendrix's set was delayed due to technical issues, but when he finally took the stage in the early hours of the morning, he delivered a powerful and electric performance. The newer material he played included "Freedom" and "Ezy Ryder." His guitar playing was virtuosic and inventive, showcasing his signature blend of blues, rock, and psychedelia.

One of the highlights was his rendition of "The Star-Spangled Banner," which he had famously performed at Woodstock the previous year.

The Isle of Wight Festival was one of his last major live shows before his death just a few weeks later. It has since become a legendary moment in rock history, and many consider it to be one of the greatest live performances ever captured on film.

Fillmore East
December 31, 1969, and January 1, 1970

Jimi Hendrix played at the Fillmore East in New York City on numerous occasions. But his shows at the Fillmore East on New Year's Eve and Day 1970 are considered some of his most powerful and innovative performances. He experimented with new sounds and styles, moving away from the psychedelic rock of his earlier work and delving deeper into the realms of funk, soul, and blues. He also was backed by a new group, Band of Gypsys, featuring bassist Billy Cox and drummer Buddy Miles.

Hendrix played extended improvisational solos, blending different styles and genres into a unique and compelling sound. The standout songs include "Machine Gun," "Who Knows," and "Power of Soul."

Notably, the shows took place just a few months before his tragic death, making them some of his final performances. Additionally, they were recorded and released as a live album, *Band of Gypsys*, which remains a classic and influential recording among fans and musicians. The shows were a defining moment in his career and a testament to his creativity and musical genius. They remain a landmark in the history of rock music and a source of inspiration for generations of musicians.

Woodstock Music and Art Fair
August 15–17, 1969

Jimi Hendrix's performance at the Woodstock festival in 1969 is one of the most famous moments in rock music history. Hendrix was the final performer, taking the stage on Monday morning after a long weekend of music.

As with his other shows, Hendrix's set was a mix of covers and original songs. However, it was his rendition of "The Star-Spangled Banner" that truly stole the show. Hendrix's intense and psychedelic guitar interpretation of the National Anthem has become legendary and is considered a defining moment of the counterculture movement of the 1960s.

The performance was also notable for its technical difficulties. The festival's sound system had been damaged by rain, and Hendrix's set was delayed for several hours while it was repaired. Despite these challenges, Hendrix and his band delivered an unforgettable performance that cemented his status as a rock 'n' roll icon.

The impact of Hendrix's Woodstock performance cannot be overstated. It was a defining moment of the festival and a cultural touchstone for a generation. His use of distortion and feedback in his guitar playing influenced countless musicians who followed, and his performance at Woodstock remains one of the most celebrated and influential moments in rock history.

Royal Albert Hall
February 18, 1968

Jimi Hendrix's concert at the Royal Albert Hall in London in 1969 was a killer show. The concert was part of The Experience's U.K. tour, and it was recorded for a live album release.

Hendrix's setlist included "Purple Haze," "Voodoo Child," and "Hey Joe," as well as a cover of Cream's "Sunshine of Your Love." The performance showcased Hendrix's incredible guitar skills as he delivered extended improvisational solos throughout the set.

The Royal Albert Hall concert is notable for several reasons. It was the first time Hendrix played in the iconic venue, which is known for its acoustics and grandeur. Additionally, Hendrix's performance was enhanced by the presence of a horn section, which added an extra dimension to his music.

The concert was a critical and commercial success, with many praising Hendrix's electrifying performance and the band's tight musicianship. A live album, *Live at Royal Albert Hall*, was released later that year and remains popular among Hendrix fans.

Monterey International Pop Festival
June 16–18, 1967

Hendrix, who was relatively unknown in the U.S. at the time, blew away the Monterey Pop audience with his electrifying performance, which included his signature guitar-burning act during "Wild Thing." His setlist included covers of "Hey Joe" and "Wild Thing," as well as "Purple Haze" and "The Wind Cries Mary."

Hendrix's performance here helped to propel him to international fame. It was also a significant moment for the festival itself, which helped to launch the careers of many legendary musicians and bands, such as Janis Joplin and The Who.

In addition to his incredible guitar playing, Hendrix's appearance and style made an impression. He wore a colorful shirt, beads, and a headband, which became his signature look.

Maui
July 30, 1970

Jimi Hendrix's performances in Maui, Hawaii, in 1970 were part of a brief but important chapter in his career. The sets were filmed, and the footage was later released as the film *Rainbow Bridge*. An accompanying soundtrack album, which featured mostly instrumental tracks, was released as well.

The Maui shows were initially intended to be part of a film project called *Rainbow Bridge Vibratory Color/Sound Experiment*, which aimed to explore the spiritual and artistic dimensions of the counterculture movement. Hendrix was approached to provide music for the film and agreed to participate, despite being in the midst of personal and professional turmoil.

249

The Maui sets were performed on the slopes of Haleakalā, a dormant volcano, and featured Hendrix performing alongside an ensemble of musicians that included Mitch Mitchell on drums, Billy Cox on bass, and Juma Sultan and Larry Lee on percussion. The shows are notable for their relaxed, improvisational feel and their emphasis on Hendrix's guitar playing.

Acknowledgments

— Dave Weiner, for introducing me to the world of publishing.

— Anthony Ziccardi, for his commitment to this book.

— My daughter Audrey, for finding the "lost" Hendrix photos in our attic.

— My daughter Kathryn, for her support.

— Henry Mayers

— Anthony Gentile

— Calvin Ross

— Pete Klasko

— Six Figure Club.com

— Jacob Hoye

— Paul Almond

— Thanks to Michael Viapiana for getting all the photos together.

— Thanks to Chris Epting for keeping it all on track.

— And to Jimi Hendrix. Thank you, wherever you are...

About the Authors

Jonathan Stathakis began his career in film and tv as a writer for numerous television specials, series and films that began with his late 1960's indie film he wrote that caused Jimi Hendrix to seek him out. He has created, produced and written a number of TV series, specials and movies for Starz, Showtime, HBO and others. Jonathan has worked with Robert Evans, Anthony Quinn, Pat Robertson, Christopher Walken, Count Basie, The Neville Brothers and many others, winning numerous awards.

Mr. Stathakis was a professional photographer, shooting iconographic photographs at Woodstock and many MTV concert events. Some of his studio shots of Jimi Hendrix appear in the book. Mr. Stathakis was awarded a Silver Award from the International Society of Photographers, and an Editor's Published Photographer Award in 2007. Mr. Stathakis has traveled the world but recently returned to his roots. He lives near the ocean on the Jersey Shore.

Chris Epting is an award-winning journalist and the author of over forty books including memoirs co-written with the Doobie Brothers, John Oates, Phil Collen, Dave Mason, and many others.